ISBN 978-1-333-82844-8
PIBN 10549352

1 MONTH OF
FREE
READING

at
www.ForgottenBooks.com

By purchasing this book you are eligible for one month membership to ForgottenBooks.com, giving you unlimited access to our entire collection of over 1,000,000 titles via our web site and mobile apps.

To claim your free month visit:
www.forgottenbooks.com/free549352

English
Français
Deutsche
Italiano
Español
Português

www.forgottenbooks.com

Mythology Photography **Fiction**
Fishing Christianity **Art** Cooking
Essays Buddhism Freemasonry
Medicine **Biology** Music **Ancient
Egypt** Evolution Carpentry Physics
Dance Geology **Mathematics** Fitness
Shakespeare **Folklore** Yoga Marketing
Confidence Immortality Biographies
Poetry **Psychology** Witchcraft
Electronics Chemistry History **Law**
Accounting **Philosophy** Anthropology
Alchemy Drama Quantum Mechanics
Atheism Sexual Health **Ancient History**
Entrepreneurship Languages Sport
Paleontology Needlework Islam
Metaphysics Investment Archaeology
Parenting Statistics Criminology
Motivational

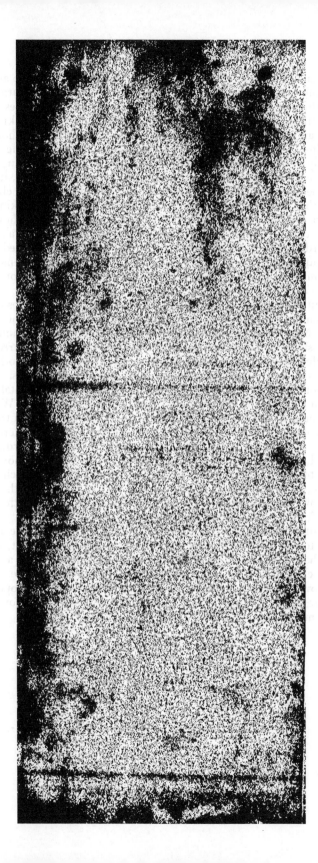

Hence the apparently wonderful facility with which the author compiles these novels. The experience of a whole life furnished Fielding with the characters and incidents of Tom Jones; but traditions and ballads of old times supply the " Great Unknown" with ample materials for this kind of writing. The very notes to Walter Scott's different poems, contain a mass of border lore, amply sufficient for half a-dozen novels like "Guy Mannering" and " Rob Roy." If there be any exception to these remarks, it is in " The Heart of Mid Lothian," which presents to us two characters that belong to all times, and are perfect in their kind : I mean old Davie Deanes and his daughter Jeanie. They are sufficient to redeem all the old half-bred witches, and half-bred wizards, in the whole series, and possess an interest derived from the purest springs of nature and probability, far more intense and legitimate than all the rest of these extravagant creations of ignorance and superstition.

But with all these drawbacks, if such they be in the eyes of the present age, the Great Unknown is still a pearl among swine. He and Miss Edgeworth are the twin stars of Bœotia, and not only shine by their own light, but by the reflection of surrounding darkness. The one, as a painter of life as it is, the other of life as it was, is without a rival in the present times. The author of Waverley is a great second-hand artist ; a capital pencil in copying old pictures, and colouring them afresh. What I particularly commend him for is, that though a friend to the government, he does not think it necessary to *cant*. There is a glow of vigourous freshness about him, so different from the faded, sickly, green and yellow tribes of cotemporary novelists, that to read one of his tales, is like contemplating a rich landscape, with the flowers of the spring, and the dews of the clear mellow morning, blooming and glittering upon it, and the pure and fragrant breeze playing in our faces.

But I cannot help thinking it is placing him where he ought not to be, to put him on a level with Fielding, Smollett, Goldsmith and Miss Edgeworth. He belongs, I imagine, to a different class of beings ; to a class of authors, who, when the charm of novelty expires, and curiosity is satisfied in the developement of the story, will never be much relished or sought after for other and more lasting beauties.

SHACKELL AND ARROWSMITH, JOHNSON'S-COURT, FLEET-STREET.

TRAVELS

IN

THE COUNTRIES

BETWEEN

ALEXANDRIA AND PARÆTONIUM,

The Lybian Desert,

SIWA, EGYPT, PALESTINE, AND SYRIA,

IN 1821.

By DR. JOHN MARTIN AUGUSTUS SCHOLZ,

Professor of Divinity in the University of Bonn.

LONDON:

PUBLISHED BY SIR RICHARD PHILLIPS & Co.

BRIDE-COURT, BRIDGE-STREET.

1822.

LONDON:

SHACKELL AND ARROWSMITH, JOHNSON'S-COURT.

INTRODUCTION.

THE resolution to undertake a journey to the East, was the most prompt and the most fortunate that I ever took. Knowing that a party of learned travellers intended to visit Cyrene, Abyssinia, Arabia, Chaldea, and Assyria; and that Baron Niebuhr, Privy Counsellor of State, and especially General Baron Von Minutoli, would provide the necessary means, I did not hesitate a moment to join them. What could in fact be more alluring, than the hope of seeing countries renowned in ancient times for their active, ingenious, and enlightened inhabitants; to explore their remaining monuments, the view of which instructs us in their works and their character; to investigate the state of the country and of the present inhabitants, the knowledge of which, is of such importance in the study of antiquity? I was, indeed, destitute of the necessary resources; but hope winged my steps, and fortune, which had attended me in my travels in southern Germany, Switzerland, France, England, and Italy, smiled also on my present undertaking. The liberality of his Royal Highness Prince Henry, and that of the Consul General Bertoldi, supplied my pecuniary wants, and obliging individuals in the East, afforded me literary assistance.

TRAVELS

IN THE COUNTRIES BETWEEN

ALEXANDRIA AND PARÆTONIUM,

THE LYBIAN DESERT, &c.

IN 1821.

———

In the beginning of August we sailed in an Austrian brigantine from Trieste for Alexandria. The country of Istria, which is seen from the sea, is among the finest in Europe; and the beautiful towns and villages with which the hills and valleys are covered, indicate a high degree of prosperity. Most of the captains of the Austrian ships, now about 1,500 in number, and their crews, are from that country, Dalmatia, Ragusa, and Cataro. The islands, between which we sailed for several days, are very well cultivated. The language of their inhabitants is the Illyrian; but each has some peculiarity in their manners, customs and dress. The inhabitants of the neighbouring continent have nearly lost these, and their language is much disfigured by a mixture of the Italian, which is very generally spoken and written in all the districts. In Trieste they for the most part speak Italian, but in the environs a dialect which seems to be between the Italian and Illyrian. The farther you go from Trieste into the interior, the purer is the language, and in Bosnia and Ragusa the best Illyrian is spoken. In Ragusa they praise the times of the republic, when they merely sent an annual present to the Sultan, their patron, and for this, carried on with five or six hundred merchantmen, under the Turkish flag, the most considerable trade in the Mediterranean; as the Venetians in the bays on this coast, where there were no duties to pay, and where a fleet stationed in them diffused life and activity, had a profitable share in the monopoly enjoyed by some cities in the Mediterranean. The dissatisfaction of the inhabitants of the Schismatic Greek church, to which three-fourths of them belong, with their present condition, is increased by the interference of the government in the pay of their bishop, who lives at Sebeniko; and who is therefore considered as dependent on it, and hence suspected. The present bishop is from Bosnia, appointed by Marshal Marmont, who is immediately under the patriarch of Constantinople, and nominates to the parishes and other benefices, either pupils educated at the seminary at Sebeniko, or monks from the Basilian convents at Castel Nuovo, Zara, and Venice. The hatred of all the diocesans, i. e. Dalmatians and Bocchese, towards the excellent bishop Kalewietz, is manifested not only in their contempt of him on his visitation of the churches, but even by an attempt on his life some years ago, on the road from Zara to Sebeniko, when his carriage was fired into, and some persons in it killed. During our twelve days' stay we made several excursions. The Catholics have, as well at Castel Nuovo as at Cataro, a Franciscan and Capuchin convent, besides the cathedral in Cataro, and the parish churches in this capital, Perasto, Dobrota, and Castel Nuovo, and when the bishopric of Cataro is vacant, they are under the Bishop of Zara.

The right of retaliation is often exercised in the most cruel manner by the offended family against the offender or his relations, as it is in the Bannat, Bosnia, Albania, Moldavia, Wallachia, and in the East. They wear the national Sclavonian dress, are generally armed, but without endangering the public safety, as the plundering Montenegrines do, and custom has preserved what originated in necessity. They are obstinate, addicted to spirituous liquors, fond of liberty, and attached to religious prejudices: the Greeks are constantly at variance with the Catholics, and all live chiefly by commerce.

After sailing from this place the wind was constantly favourable, and we saw at a distance the coast of Albania, the Ionian Islands, and the Morea, which I visited on my return. In 36 deg. 12 min. N. latitude, about thirty leagues from the coast of the Morea, on the twenty-ninth of August, at half-past one P. M. while we were all standing on deck, we felt a trembling motion of the ship, which seemed to be caused by an earthquake, and lasted about half a minute. We had a slight north wind, but the sea was high, the sky clear, and the thermometer at 25 deg. in the sun. The captain of a ship from Trieste, whom I met with at Alexandria, told me, that he had observed similar phenomena three times in the summer, always near the coast of Sicily, but in a much greater degree, so that wine glasses were overturned. Except some optical illusions we saw nothing remarkable. The north-west wind predominated, and the night dew was very heavy. We saw but few fish, birds very rarely, and insects only when the wind blew from the shore. We were frequently impatient at the delay, proceeding from the custom of the captains on these coasts, of stopping, sometimes for a month together, with their relations; but it gave us an opportunity of becoming acquainted with a nation whose manners and customs resemble those of the East more than of the West. On the 15th of August a great festival was celebrated at Madonna della Neve, and Catholics, Greeks, and Turks flocked from the Bays of Ragusa, from Bosnia, and Albania, to the miraculous image, on an island near Perasto. The inhabitants of these bays once formed a number of small republics, which depended on the Emperors of Byzantium. The dominion of the Spaniards is recalled to mind by the Castel Spagnolo, on the highest point, near Castel Nuovo; that of the Knights of Malta, by several buildings erected by them; that of the Turks, by the city walls, and some Arabic inscriptions; that of the Venetians, by the fortifications above the town of Cataro, and the visit of the Russians, English, Montenegrines, and French, by the remains of houses which were burned by them to no purpose, and the ruined prosperity of the whole country.

On the 3d of September we arrived at Alexandria. The first question we put to the two pilots who came to steer us into the port, was, whether the plague was in Alexandria? They assured us that there had been no death for a month past, and the city is generally free from July to October inclusive. There were about three hundred ships in the old harbour, the greater part Turkish, about fifty Austrian, ten Sardinian, and a few French, English, Swedish, Danish, and Neapolitan. In the dangerous new harbour, to which all the vessels of the Franks were formerly compelled to repair, there were only sixteen Turkish ships. As we were going on shore we met several seamen in boats, who saluted us, and bellowed out their monotonous Arabic songs. At the custom-house the Arabs fought together for our things, every one desiring to earn something by carrying them. The entrance into the African town is highly interesting to a stranger, from the novelty it presents to him. The crowd of Arabs, one dressed in rags, another in a long Oriental dress, all with beards and dark brown complexions, most of them extremely miserable, the great number of hollow-eyed half-naked children, running all day long about the streets, and calling out *Jaallah,* the pale, yellow, bloated women, with their eyes sunk in their heads, their faces covered with rags, in a detestable dress, and creeping about like ghosts, are but melancholy objects. We saw burying grounds with an infinite number of tablets with inscriptions, women lamenting over the graves of their friends, and an army of dogs, which furiously attacked us, and pursued us till we were out of their district. We went to the quarter of the Franks, where we

were received in the most friendly manner. We made ourselves
acquainted with the city and its environs, with the manners and
customs of the East, and prepared for our intended expedition into the Cyrenaica.

A company of well prepared travellers could not certainly have
selected a more interesting excursion for their first attempt, than
into the territory of Cyrene. This country was almost forgotten.
The captains of vessels, who sometimes went to Derna and Bengasi, to fetch the produce, heard of an ancient desolate city on
the heights, commanding the whole country, but paid no attention to it, or to the engraved stones found there, which the Bedouins offered them for trifles. Physicians, who accompanied the
Dey of Tripoli in his campaigns against the Bedouins of that
district, and the inhabitants of Fezzan, spoke of it, but only in
general terms; and Della Cella was the first who noticed the importance of researches in this country, to the arts, history, and
philology. The desolate country between Derna and Bengasi,
offered to the captains of vessels, that came in the Summer from
Malta, Alexandria, and Candia, abundance of horned cattle,
sheep, and fruits; and their wool is thought equal to the best in
Barbary. What treasures may the gardens of the Hesperides,
the beautiful meadows of Ericab, the populous Pentapolis, and
above all, Cyrene, have contained? Many celebrated nations of
the interior resorted hither, and Phœnicians, Egyptians, Greeks,
and Carthaginians, brought immense riches to this spot, to purchase its productions, its engraved stones, and, above all, the juice
prepared from the sylphium; and Cyrene, as a Phœnician, Athe-
nian, Egyptian, and Roman colony, rivalled the parent cities in
the splendor of its works of art, and in luxury. How many
monuments and inscriptions of those various periods may there
be in Cyrene; what treasures of this description in the ruins of
Berenice, Teuchira, Ptolemais, Barca, and Apollonia? The
way we had resolved to take through the district of Mareotis, by
Apis and Paraetonium, and the return by the Oases of Augela,
and Siwa, is highly interesting to the antiquarian, and those
places are not so well known as they deserve to be. As it
seemed hazardous to begin our travels in the East with so expensive an expedition, without a previous sufficient knowledge
of the language and manners of the country, and without carefully weighing all the circumstances, well meaning friends ad-
vised us to initiate ourselves at a smaller expence. This country
is besides known to be one of the most dangerous, on account of
the attacks of the Bedouins, so that scarcely a month passes in
which caravans are not plundered and murdered. At Siwa we saw
the remains of an unfortunate caravan of eighteen persons, who,
with forty camels, were going from Siwa to Bengasi, but were

attacked four days journey beyond Siwa, and after the danger
was past had fled back to Siwa.   The inconceivable sufferings
and hardships, especially on their return, had deprived them of
their understanding, and they were hardly able to speak.   Suc-
cess cannot be obtained without profound knowledge of the inhabitants, rare sagacity, and indefatigable efforts. Lastly, care in
the choice of the season of the year is requisite. The great loss
of time caused by the heavy and continual rains in the winter
months is not to be compared with the inconveniences of the heat
in the other part of the year ; and the antiquarian, and still more
the naturalist, will best commence his researches, when we, according to our calculation, should long since have ended them :
but the hope of being useful to science, and of showing our
gratitude to our patrons, made us overlook every difficulty. The
company consisted of General Baron Minutoli, M. Liemann,
Professor of Architecture, Messrs. Ehrenberg and Hemprich,
Doctors of Physic and Naturalists, and Doctor and Professor
Aug. Scholz. There were besides three assistants of the General, an assistant of the Naturalists', two Dragomans, and some
Arab servants.

   We set out on the 5th of October, proceeding westwards, at
the distance of a quarter of a league to three leagues from the sea
coast, and arrived on the 25th at the well of Chaur.   Part of our
caravan, viz. the General and his attendants, the first Dragoman,
and the Sheik, or chief of our Bedouins, left us here, and returned to Cairo, while the other part advanced to the Tripolitan
territory, where it waited from the 28th of October to the 14th of
November for permission to continue the journey, and an escort,
from the Bey of Bengasi.   The caravan seemed to be judiciously
arranged under the protection of Mehemet Ali Pacha, and the
direction of experienced men, and to encourage the fondest
hopes. Hadsch Hendawi Abu Daheb, a considerable Sheik of the
horde Dschimeat, and twenty-five armed Bedouins, with thirty-
six camels, were hired to defend the company, and convey their
provisions, clothes, and books, and were answerable for their
safety. The good understanding between Mehemet Ali and the
Pacha of Tripoli, and his relationship with the Bey of Bengasi,
were well calculated to inspire them with confidence in his pressing recommendations, and to quiet their apprehensions of the ex-
cesses of the Bedouins, who dread his powerful arm : under
these circumstances we overlooked the disputes with the Bedouins
before we left Alexandria, not considering that they might be the
prelude of more serious ones in the desert. Promises were extorted from them, which the Bedouin readily makes in hopes of
gain, but interprets at his pleasure, and breaks without scruple.
They promised to take fodder for the camels with them, to travel

the more quickly, but let them graze when opportunity offered, in spite of all our remonstrances. We paid for three camels to carry water, but they generally went without, because they would bring us to wells, the situation of which they did not know, which contained salt water, or perhaps did not exist at all. The Sheik not only did as he pleased in this respect, but left the caravan at will, to visit his friends in the neighbourhood. The licentiousness of the Bedouins then knew no bounds; and on one occasion they caused us no small embarrassment. Some of them stole a goat, and the owners pursued them. Every one prepared to defend himself, in expectation of an attack, which we feared would be seconded by some horsemen at a distance ; our apprehensions were however groundless, but the Bedouins availed themselves of this opportunity to provoke and vex us. Our camels, which otherwise ran dispersed, were driven together; the Bedouins marched in battle array, and fired with ball in every direction. The engaged to take us the right way; but confessed they wantedya guide, whom the company should pay. But nothing was more disagreeable than the slow progress of our caravan in a desolate country. Our Dragomans too were not qualified for their task, and often caused us much trouble. Nothing was more unpleasant than to have to converse with the Bedouins through them, convinced that we should but half attain our object, or perhaps not at all ; and the complaints made in the East of the insolence, stupidity, and malicious impositions of this class of men, are as just as they are general. The most abominable acts of injustice are practised by them, especially at Constantinople, where they are ranked with fire and the plague, as one of the three greatest punishments which afflict the capital of the Turkish empire. I endeavoured to fill up the time by excursions on foot in all directions, especially towards the sea coast, though there was some danger of straying from the caravan, and losing my way in the desert. The weather was favourable ; the sky generally serene and the horizon clear: when this was not the case, the groups of clouds, especially at sun-rise or sun-set, presented a most beautiful and sublime sight. The night dews were more or less considerable, according to the violence of the wind, but always injurious to the naked eye. We had rain on four days only, and on the 2d of November, in the afternoon, a thunder storm, that came up from the east, but without rain. The air at this season is pure and healthy, though damp. The temperature varied from 10 deg. to 25 deg. of heat at noon : the nights were generally cool, the north and north-west winds predominated, which increased the coolness of the nights.

On the 26th, 27th, 28th, and 30th of October, and the 1st, 3d, 4th, and 5th of November, the violent *chamise* (west wind) gave

us all head-aches and oppression on the chest, and its gusts threatened destruction to the eyes. It announced its coming by a very
fiery red the evening before, was stormy, whirled up the sand,
and piled immense masses of clouds towards the north. In
November meteors in the north-east were frequent, which, like
the aurora borealis, illumed the gloomy nights for hours together.
The tides are almost imperceptible along the whole coast; but
when the wind is high, the waves wet the sand to the distance of
several hundred paces, so that it is thus bleached beautifully
white, and forms a singular contrast with that at a distance. As
it rains only in three months, and for the rest of the year the sun
scorches the plain, which has no protection from its beams, nature
may be said to live only in these three months. In them the plants
shoot, blossom, and fade; the animals copulate and increase; and
after they are passed, most of them hasten to the sleep of death.

It was easy to perceive that the division of the company would
ruin the whole enterprise. The letters of recommendation, &c.
were calculated for one chief person, who, as the friend of the
Pacha, gave consistency and unity to the caravan, and could promote its objects by large presents. If he withdrew, success was
very doubtful, even with the greatest sacrifices of money and
labour, and we might fail even under the most favourable circumstances. The company, however, resolved not to neglect the
faint hope that remained, and to wait twenty days, for the answer
to the letters which had been sent by sea and land, to ask permission, and an escort for the journey. It may seem strange, that
after such great sacrifices we had not the courage to follow the
advice of the Arabs, to advance without permission, and atone by
presents for the violation of Oriental etiquette; or that we en-
trusted the most important concerns to the Bedouins, who deceived us, and every day, after holding council, tormented
us with vexatious proposals, sometimes desiring to return for
want of provisions, sometimes to advance over the frontiers,
hourly announcing new dangers, and trying to make our abode in
a very critical situation still more painful. At length, after long
waiting to no purpose, we resolved, on the 1st of November, to
hasten southward to Siwa, where we arrived on the 18th. This
journey through the desert was fatiguing in the extreme; for
having but little water we rode for three days, twenty hours together, at a rapid pace, the camels making from eighty-five to
ninety steps in a minute, whereas in general they take only
seventy. At Siwa we were ill received by the barbarous inhabitants, treated like prisoners, and travelled on the 23d as far as
Ainelaggab, two leagues eastward from Siwa Kebir, near the great
lake which incloses the fertile Oasis of Ofen, without having seen
the principal curiosities of the Oasis. On the 25th and 26th we

were at Kara, sixteen leagues from Siwa, the 29th and 30th at Vadi Heische, twelve leagues from Kara, the 4th of December at Vadi Libbeck, seventeen leagues from Heische, the 6th and 7th at Hamam, seventeen leagues from Libbeck, and the 9th at Alexandria, sixteen leagues from Hamam. We suffered severely on this journey. The want of water and provisions obliged us to make very long stages, while the heavy rains at the beginning of December, cold north winds almost daily at the end of November and beginning of December, damp chilly nights, swarms of vermin in our linen, and a hundred other hardships, filled up the measure of our sufferings.

The death of one person of our company two days before our arrival in Alexandria, the dangerous illness of another, who likewise died soon afterwards, and the bad health of the remainder, caused the first plan to be abandoned, and it was agreed to follow the example already set by the chief person in the company, so that every one should act independently in the pursuit of his own peculiar object. M. Lieman, Professor of Architecture in the Academy of Berlin, died on the 11th of December, at ten o'clock, of a debility, caused by violent diarrhœa and fever. He was buried at half-past three o'clock the same day, in the Greek monastery.

As I should have been losing time by staying at Alexandria, where I had previously passed a month, I embarked on the Nile for Cairo. My situation made it impossible for me to undertake immediately, at this season, the journey to Upper Egypt; and I also thought it too hazardous to venture on my favourite project of a visit to Nubia and Abyssinia, before the expences were sufficiently provided for, though the Coptic Patriarch and other considerable persons at Cairo took great interest in it. A very favourable opportunity, however, offered to visit Syria and Palestine, countries which I above all desired to become acquainted with, the Bishop of Babylon having invited me to accompany him thither. This worthy prelate, a Frenchman of La Vendée, named Pierre Couperi, was going to Bagdad, which the Propaganda had assigned him for his residence, as Bishop of the Catholies of the Latin Church in the whole of the ancient Chaldea and Assyria. This see was founded by a French lady one hundred and fifty years ago, with the annexed condition that it should always be filled by a Frenchman. The Christians of the Latin rite are not above three thousand in this great diocese. The very numerous Catholics of the Chaldean rite have their patriarchs and bishops; those of the Syrian and Armenian church, and the Maronites, have also their bishops. Having viewed the curiosities of Cairo and its environs, especially the pyramids, we commenced our journey on the 5th of January. The weather was in general favourable. At Bilbeisch we were joined by a company of English; at Saalhigeh by thirty-one Coptic, Syrian, and other merchants, with twelve negro slaves, and an Indian dervise, with an attendant. He was once a rich man, who had sold his property to make a pilgrimage to Mecca and Jerusalem, and had been travelling about for four years; but having been robbed at Mecca, he now subsists upon alms. Many travellers from Bilbeisch and Gaza also joined us, so that our caravan consisted of about eighty persons, with one hundred and forty camels, and thirty asses. Beyond Arisch, where there was more security, and no want of water, they divided into several parties, some travelled all night, and all of them quicker than we did. The company was very agreeable and instructive. I learned to appreciate the good nature of the Orientals, and when the day's journey was concluded, which usually began at five in the morning, and ended at four in the afternoon, I lived among them, sitting on the ground, happier than in the tedious conversaziones of Italy. The Bedouins, whom we met on our first unfortunate expedition to the Cyrenaica, daily vexed us with forms which characterize them as Mahometans, but are odious to Christians. These merchants, though chiefly Mahometans, never ventured to touch on this point, and neglected no opportunity to make the journey agreeable, and to do us every kindness in their power; so that travelling in the East, of which my first expedition had given me so bad a specimen, became daily more interesting and useful to me. In choosing the resting place for the night, valleys are preferred, as being sheltered from the winds. We alone had tents. The Arabs, each party by itself, took their stations very irregularly, at intervals of six or eight paces, spreading their carpets on the ground; and placing the baggage in a semicircle, which served as a back for the divan, they slept in the open air, covered with their upper garments. Each party made a fire to warm themselves, and dress their repast. Most were contented with cold provisions, dates, and barley bread; some drank coffee. The camels and asses were immediately fed, generally with beans. In the evening they conversed, and went to sleep about ten o'clock. In caravans, with which I afterwards travelled, religious hymns were sung at half-past three in the morning, but by such rude voices and in such monotonous notes, that I was glad to go away sooner. This never happened here. The negro slaves danced sometimes at our request, but they were not skilful: they were well treated, and always cheerful. I travelled from Gaza to Jerusalem, thence made excursions, first along the coast into Kesserwan, then into the interior of Palestine, and returned at Easter to Jerusalem, in hopes of finding news from home. After returning from the Jordan, the pilgrims thought of their departure, contented and happy in the heavenly pleasure which they had enjoyed. I also prepared to depart, but whither? I had had my books and letters' sent from Masr to Aleppo. My first wish was to reach Damascus, near to which I had been before; but the accounts of disturbances in European Turkey, of which we had already some report in April, became daily more positive and alarming, and the fears excited by them more general, till official information and orders were received in May. All the Christians were disarmed, and they dreaded the recurrence of the scenes of horror which had accompanied the French invasion. At that time they lost their property, and many hundreds their lives, and they now trembled for the fate of all the Christians in Palestine. I hesitated about visiting Damascus, and hastened to Jaffa. Still greater consternation prevailed there. The Franks had suffered here also by the arrogance of the Turks: English travellers were disarmed at Rama, the Russian consul expelled from his house and plundered. This was no inviting prospect for me. I was affected the most by news from Acre, stating that all the poor had been expelled from the town, the Russian and Austrian flags on the consuls' houses, cut down, and Katafalko, the consul, murdered in prison.

I here wrote on the 8th of May a letter to my uncle, from which the following is an extract: " You have learned by preceding letters the cause and the manner of my coming to Palestine. In February I accompanied the Bishop of Babylon from Jerusalem to Acre. On my way thither I examined the beautiful plain of Sarona, Cesarea, Tantora, and Atlid, and made excursions from Acre to Mount Carmel and all Galilee. On my return through Galilee, to be at Jerusalem at Easter, I became acquainted with Samaria, but with imminent danger of my life. With some English travellers I rode along the Jordan at the time when pilgrims visit it, to Richa on the Dead Sea, and Mount Karantan. I had previously visited Saba, Bethania, and the other remarkable places in Judea ; I now wished to go through Samaria and the Decapolis, to Damascus and Mount Lebanon. But this journey must be made either in a large company, or in the disguise of a poor Bedouin. The former is not to be had, and the latter seemed dangerous at this period ; for what is more likely to excite suspicion than taking down detailed notes of any place and its curiosities. Exaggerated reports of the troubles in Greece and Turkey came to Jerusalem, and nothing less was talked of than war between Austria and Russia and the Sultan. I therefore hastened to Jaffa, to convey my manuscripts, ancient coins, antiquities, and books, to Cyprus, and thence send them to Trieste. Jaffa is now full of pilgrims, the roofs are crowded with them. The songs of the Arnauts, the discord of which is lost in the roaring of the sea, dispels my melancholy ; but the arrogance of the Turks is intolerable. Formerly I was fond of entering into conversation with them ; now I cannot bear to look at them. I am grieved when I see them brandish their pistols round the heads of the poor Christians, and terrify them till they are ready to sink into the earth. But the day of deliverance for me and for many thousands is at hand. Twenty large vessels and thirty-five smaller ones are ready to receive the pilgrims.—I have not yet any good news from home : you see therefore that a prolongation of the two years leave of absence is not to be thought of. I must have returned before, had I not been fortunate in meeting with such good company to travel with, &c."

I wrote the following letter to my mother :

" Thus then I have ended my pilgrimage in the Holy Land. I have followed the steps of the holy family from the birth of our Lord in Bethlehem, to his circumcision, on their flight to Egypt, and in their domestic life in Galilee. I have traced our Saviour's public life in Samaria and Judea; frequently visited in particular the scene of the last events of his life ; added my tears to those of his disciples and friends, as millions of pilgrims have done, who before me had sought consolation and comfort on the spot where the Saviour suffered death on the cross for the human race. My happiness was above all earthly feeling, when I was absolved from past transgressions, where the Saviour of the world himself promised forgiveness of sins, and partook of the body of the Lord, where he himself instituted the holy sacrament. How often did I place m self in the situation of his mother, when she saw her beloved son, here die the most cruel death, there glorified in transcendant majesty as the Saviour of mankind. The fancy here draws a living picture which becomes for ever her property, because we are most deeply sensible what life is, when we behold in spirit so great an example before us, when we boldly look into futurity to which the Man-God himself opened us the way, and in the joyful triumph of confidence and hope, exclaim with the apostle, ' O Death, where is thy sting ! O Grave, where is thy victory !' "

The reasons above stated decided my departure from Syria in the middle of May ; for to continue my travels was impossible. Travelling in the East is troublesome even in time of peace ; in company this is not so much felt, but if you are alone, you are at the mercy of the mule driver. If he is a Mahometan you must not reply to his abuse, and can never threaten him without danger. If he is a Christian you are the more exposed to the insults of the Mahometans. The traveller often suffers by their conventions with each other, or their customs. Thus, on the way from Jerusalem to Acre, we had scarcely gone a league, when a

troop of Arabs suddenly came forward, threw the burdens from
the mules, and stoned and beat the owners. We asked the
cause, but no one answered. We were going to turn back, when
the *Abrigos* and the Vice-Procurator of the Latin council, the
first going to Jerusalem, the second to Jaffa, came up, and decided in favour of our Arabs, the assailants, as we now learned,
having claimed the profit to be made by this journey. On some
occasions they broke the most solemn engagements for the hire of
mules, exacting more than was stipulated, demanding payment
for services never performed, or for articles never supplied ; and
one of them, whose unjust demands had been resisted, run after
me in the streets of Acre, and related to all the Mahometans,
with tears in his eyes, how unjustly an infidel had treated him.

At Nazareth I agreed with a Greek to conduct me through
Samaria to Jerusalem for thirty-five piastres. At Dschenin he
heard there was danger, and refused to proceed on the journey.
All dissuaded me, but I persisted, and was forced to engage a
Sheik to go with me, for a large sum, who could give and return
the Mahometan salutation, " Salam Alaikum." But these and similar unpleasant scenes are not to be compared with what the
Franks have lately experienced. A Piedmontese Count paid
five hundred piastres for the journey from Nazareth to Dscheras, (a
journey of two days and a half), and was plundered notwithstand-
ing. A company of English wished to go from Damascus to Tad-
mor. They paid the Sheik half of his reward (five hundred
piastres) before hand, and made him large presents; when they
had travelled some days, a messenger came to meet them, with
the news, that it was dangerous to proceed; the Bedouins being
in insurrection. The Sheik declared he could not answer for
their lives, but would do his utmost to serve them. They were
obliged to give up their expedition, and to lose their seven
or eight hundred piastres. Some other Englishmen had hired
camels for two months, and paid beforehand, for a journey to
Upper Egypt. On the way the driver became ill, the camels
would not go on, and they were happy to return by another
opportunity. At Naplous, the face of an Englishman was cleft
in two, in the court-yard of the Motsallem; because in a dispute
with his conductor he had abused a soldier. An Englishman returning from Richa, was plundered and left naked, and a cripple.
His conductor had run away.—These mule drivers generally ask
ten times as much of the Franks as of natives. The terms are
fixed by the Dragomans, who are liberal at other people's expence, even when they get nothing by it. Rich Englishmen
have done much injury to other travellers: they come with some
thousands of pounds sterling, and he who does not pay like them,
is pitied as a poor devil not worth attending to. The fathers in

the Holy Land are accused, but wrongfully, of favouring these extortions: but the servants in the convents are uncommonly insolent. Thus I have seen them wait whole days at the door of a traveller, for a large douceur, (Bakschisch,) because they have put him in mind of a festival in the church. This selfish character, this intolerable importunity, is become contagious. The Armenian and Greek monks have a genteel mode of indemnifying themselves for services performed. They do not fail to give the stranger somebody as a guide, who soon gains his confidence, and knows the tax to be paid, for benefits received; to the church ; for, according to the customary polite way of speaking, the church, and not the clergy receives it. If he is rich, this tax often amounts with the Armenians to one thousand piastres for a few dinners and nights' lodging. The Greeks ask less, but the oftener. The poor pilgrims on the other hand receive kind treatment from them. They give them little, but that little as long as they need it. The Latins maintain them very well for a month ; but when that is expired they must go away. In the observance of this, otherwise good rule, they have often laid aside all Christian charity, and committed cruelties which will be an eternal disgrace to the intercessors of the Catholics at the tomb of Christ, and may serve as an illustration of the history of the degenerate monastic spirit, for this was not the intention of St. Francis. They have cast poor half naked pilgrims into the street, given them nothing on which to lay their heads, and haughtily rejected their entreaties for a bit of bread. On such acts the blessing of God will never come.—In places where there is no monastery or hospital, strangers lodge in the house of a consul, or in a khan. These are inconvenient and dirty, and men and animals are often lodged together in one stable. Those who travel with Greeks generally lodge with the Kuris, (or Greek priests), whose dwellings are in general very wretched. In summer travellers are exposed to the burning heat of the sun, in winter to torrents of rain. From the want of regular roads they are often in danger of losing their way, or in bad weather of sinking in the mud. Thus on my first journey in Galilee, my horse sunk so deep into the mud, half a league from the lake of Tiberias, that I fell off several times, and had to wade in it up to my knees. In Samaria, in the valley before the village of Taniun, several camels sunk in the mud, and the drivers had to wade up to their hips to carry their heavy burdens on to the high dry ground, and help the animals out. My mule also sunk, and we had great difficulty in getting it out. No bridges are ever built over the rivers, and wading through them is often dangerous when the waters are high.

In the cultivated parts of Syria the best mode of travelling is on mules; they carry great burdens, and go much faster than camels, which last are in general less fit for the hard rocks of Judea. They do not tread firm, and often sink under their load.

On the coast, on Mount Lebanon, and in Galilee, there is no fear of robbers; but in the other parts of Syria travelling is always dangerous. Three years ago a caravan, with more than one hundred camels, going from Damascus to Bagdad, was entirely plundered, and the people murdered. The caravans from Damascus to Aleppo are often attacked. The journey to Palmyra has become extremely dangerous for the Franks, since the Bedouins in that quarter were chastised by an army, by command of the Sultan, for the murder of an English traveller of distinction. The Nomades think themselves authorized to commit these cruelties, either because there is some person with the caravan upon whom they have to exercise the law of retaliation, or because no agreement has been made with them for the payment to which they claim a right. Frequently, however, they are impelled merely by lust of rapine and bloodshed.

Extract from another letter written from Zante to my uncle: " You have learned by my letter of the 6th of May, why I have given up my plan of going to Aleppo by way of Damascus and Lebanon. We left the roads of Jaffa sooner than I expected. As soon as the pilgrims received from the Motsallem permission to depart, and the price of the passage had been fixed by him, all hastened to the harbour. I chose an Austrian polacca, which was already hired for a part of the Russian pilgrims, eighty in number, and was to go by way of Cyprus to Constantinople. The Russian consul, who had been so ill used, was of the party, and his fear of the Turks induced the captain to cut the cable to escape without loss of time. Having a very favourable west wind, we were within forty-eight hours in sight of Cyprus. The landing there was desirable for the whole company, who in their great hurry had not been able to provide themselves with provisions; it was agreeable to the consul, who could here take measures for the better execution of his precipitate resolution; and it was most important to me, because the harbour being full of European ships I might find a conveyance to any port in the Turkish empire. At Larnaca too, the residence of some hundred Europeans and several consuls, I might hope for more protection than in Syria; and when I had attained my object in Cyprus, easily pass over to the Syrian coast, and then, if possible, undertake my journey by way of Aleppo, Mosul, Bagdad, and Arabia, to Abyssinia. But Providence had decreed otherwise. Just as we were going to land a storm drove us towards Rhodes. Various plans now occurred to me. Sometimes I thought of embarking

at Rhodes in a vessel for Cyprus; then I was for going to
Smyrna, and joining a caravan for the interior of Asia; but I
persisted in my resolution to hasten to Syria, to accomplish which
I was ready to hazard my life. A conversation with some Greek
pirates, who cruized in the channel of Rhodes, and lay in wait for
Turkish ships, did not deter me, though the accounts they gave
were by no means encouraging. According to them the Greeks
were in possession of the whole of the Morea, all the Greeks on
the islands and on the continent under arms, and a Russian and
Austrian army about to pursue the Turks to Constantinople,
where the European ministers were in the greatest danger.
Some, they said, had been ill-treated, others had fled, and all had
with difficulty escaped the most imminent danger; that an insurrection of the Greeks had become a war of the Christians
against the Mahometans. They furnished us with provisions
and wine, for which the Russian consul gave his receipt, but
warned us against visiting the city of Rhodes, because there, as
every where else on the continent of the Ottoman empire, the
Turks and Jews had vowed death and destruction to the Christians. We fled from place to place, found every where anxious
expectation, conflicting reports, no authentic information to guide
our proceedings, and no opportunity of conveyance to any great
sea-port.

In Patmos nothing was thought of but the equipment of ships;
all were eager for the war with the Turks, no sacrifice was too
great. The youth were already under arms; only old men and
women were left at home. The Morea and most of the islands
were in insurrection; combatants flocked from various parts of
the Turkish empire; Ypsilanti tried to raise Moldavia and Wallachia; all breathed revenge. The great affair of the Greek
nation now gradually unfolded itself before our eyes. The plan
for throwing off the Turkish yoke had been six years in bringing
to maturity. The secret was known only to a few, and on these
few the whole edifice reposed. Several hundred ships were built,
ammunition procured, and millions of money had been laid upon
the altar of their country by the rich Greek merchants and captains. The events in the south-west of Europe quickly matured
their plans. The movements among the nation drew attention,
and the assembling of the people excited suspicion. The divan of
Constantinople demanded an explanation, and received it. The
circumstance appeared to it of no importance; it had long since
been accustomed to treat such events with indifference. But now
reports came from all quarters; Lord Strangford, the English
Ambassador, communicated to it the whole plan of the con-
spiracy, as it had been discovered to him, from authentic sources,
by the Lord High Commissioner of the Ionian Islands. There

were traitors among the Greeks themselves. The divan, in its anger, caused many Greeks of distinction to be beheaded. The Patriarch of Constantinople was one of the first victims. Many princes, archbishops, bishops, and priests shared a similar fate. Dreadful scenes now followed in Constantinople, Smyrna, and other parts of the Turkish empire. Each party tried to destroy the other. It was a war of extermination. The Turks were cruel; but the Greeks were still more so. Many thousands of innocent people first lost their limbs, and then their lives. They triumphed over the murder of three hundred Albanians, who had fallen into their hands before Naxos, and that of the crews of many Turkish ships, and of women, children, and old men, at the taking of Athens, and other places. I could fill whole sheets with the cruelties they have committed. In Hydra, the centre of the Greek marine, we found every thing in the greatest agitation. The old government of the island had been overthrown a few days before our arrival, and the members of it, who had fled, were murdered by the people. Fugitive families from Smyrna, Macedonia, and the Morea flocked hither. All were either in extacy or profound affliction. As long as the people were not distressed and alarmed by bad news, there were festivities without end; but what availed these to the numerous families who had been forced to abandon their property. I was glad to leave this scene of confusion. I found the Ionian Islands also full of fugitive Moreotes, who had taken refuge in them. Here, under the protection of the English government, every body could speak freely of the Greeks, and the least unfortunate joined in the enthusiasm of their countrymen for religion, liberty, and their country. But it was more and more evident to me, that this enterprize did not deserve the encomiums which hitherto had been bestowed on it; and that it was rather the work of some ambitious arrogant individuals, who prepared destruction for their nation. In these islands also it is difficult to find a conveyance, and all communication is obstructed. Every ship brings fresh and more terrible accounts from various parts of the Turkish empire; and as I cannot think of pursuing my journey in it, I shall soon embark for Trieste, and then hasten to return to you.

Topography of the Country between Alexandria and the Frontiers of Tripoli.

From Alexandria westwards you go for nine leagues on the small isthmus which is formed by the Mediterranean Sea and Lake Mareotis. It is from a quarter to half a league broad, and uneven. Along the lake there is a chain of hills of limestone, like a dam, which extends still farther to the tower of the Arabs and Abousir. On the two shores is sand, in the middle sand or clay, and some salt plains. Near Marabut and Mikzan there are gardens, and here and there arable land. Behind Abousir there are several chains of hills, consisting either of clay or sandstone, which run westward, sometimes parallel, a quarter or half a league from each other, sometimes confounded together; they are either bare, or, like the plains and valleys, covered with clay or sand; there are likewise several groups of hills. Elgaibe, whose highest mountain, Dschebel Meriam, is about eight hundred feet, is undoubtedly the loftiest and most extensive of the whole coast. The further you go from the sea the more the land rises from the beach, till, at the distance of from ten to fifteen leagues an innumerable quantity of sand-hills, alternate with ridges of quartz, full of petrifactions and limestones, with extensive plains, form here and there fertile valleys. In these, shelter from the scorching beams of the sun may generally be found under bushes, which cannot be had in an immense plain where there is neither house, nor tree, nor shrub; sometimes refreshment is afforded by a well or a cistern, with spring or rain water, and at times even in a straw hut, the dwelling of a numerous family, with their domestic animals.

From Abousir to two leagues behind Senetzerk, sandstone predominates, and then clay and limestone. Where there is sand the shore seems to gain more and more upon the sea; for at the distance of fifteen to twenty paces from the water, masts and planks of ships are found buried in the sand. Hence no trace is to be discerned of most of the harbours on this coast celebrated in ancient history. Near it there are salt plains, brackish springs and wells, the latter of which seem to contain much natron. I saw the most in the neighbourhood of Lamaid, and two leagues from Agaba, and at the latter place a salt lake a league in length and a quarter of a league in breadth. This tract contains a great many cisterns, which are of the highest importance in a country where rain is to be expected only at the end of November, December, and January, and the beginning of February, and where springs are rare. At all times, especially under the Saracens, the making of such cisterns was considered as a meritorious work. Their size and construction are very various, round, angular, equilateral, roughly hewn in the stone, or carefully lined with a mixture of lime and sand. Some derive their names from those who erected them, others from their situation; for instance, *Dokan,* as lying in a spot encompassed by hills, and, like the wells, they have given their names to the places where they are situated. Most of them are ruined or neglected, and it is only near the wells that some inhabitants still dwell with their flocks; tracts of country, many square leagues in extent, full of fine vegetation, are desolate for

want of population. On the isthmus, the wells of Marabut on the
sea-coast, two leagues from Kereir, and Mizan, on the sea-coast,
seven leagues and a half from Alexandria, are the principal. Beyond Abousir, for the distance of eighty-two leagues, there are
numerous wells, some filled with rain, and some with brackish
water. Most of them are deep, but greatly dilapidated. Near
them are stone troughs, and in the morning we often found them
surrounded by flocks. They are mostly in low plains, and much
vegetation near them.

Thus, on a tract of coast, eighty-four leagues in length, and
from ten to fifteen leagues in breadth, we find neither mountain
nor river, wood nor village; only hollows, low hills, and slopes
occasionally intersect the wearisome plain, and when you have
ascended one of these, another endless plain, with similar objects,
opens to your view. The caravans, the flocks of sheep, and herds
of camels, that now and then pass by, alone recall to mind the existence of men, or the barking of a dog announces the neighbourhood of an encampment: the same may be said of the almost
equally extensive tract from Agaba to Derna.

The nature of the soil is not unfavourable to agriculture. To
the distance of one-eighth, or a quarter of a league from the sea,
it is sandy or rocky; thence to the distance of ten or fifteen
leagues inland it is clayey, and rarely sand or stone. Yet it is
only in a small part of it that barley is sown in December. They
slightly turn up the ground with a small rake fastened to a camel,
throw in the seed, and cover it. In three months they pluck off
the ears, and thrash out the grain upon the field. They do not
understand either agriculture or gardening. The vegetation
affords excellent and abundant pasture to the herds of the frugal
inhabitants. The shrubs grow in the long and narrow hollows
which are here and there met with in all directions, and have
been formed by torrents of water. The most beautiful green
is often found in them, while around them every thing is scorched
and withered, and Nature seems to be dead. Trees are very
rare in this district. Though the country appears poor in insects
in October,—(we saw none in great numbers except ants, flies,
dragon flies, a few species of beetles, and moths, and particularly
the *scarabæus sacer*), it is probably very rich in winter. The
snails of the desert cling in some places to the earth and the
plants, as sea-shells to the rocks and the coast. The great quantity of coral dust, shells, snails, and fungi, which are seen on the
beach, of different sizes, forms, and colours, shew that the sea is
full of inhabitants. Various kinds of lizards, adders, and serpents, of an ash grey colour, creep upon the earth; while birds
of prey, such as eagles, vultures, and owls, marsh fowl, and singing birds, especially many ubaras, fill the air. The birds of prey

live in the clefts of the rocks. The Bedouins are very skilful in training a kind of falcon for the chace, not only of birds, but also of hares and gazelles, which they generally kill without lacerating them. For a well-trained bird of this kind they pay fifty Spanish piasters.

Rats, hares, gazelles, foxes, and wolves are the most common quadrupeds. The doméstic animals of the inhabitants are camels, sheep, goats, asses, horses, cows, and dogs: the camel is indisputably the most useful. They employ these animals in agriculture, and in removing their tents and effects; they let them to caravans, and use their milk, flesh, and skin, without any expence for their maintenance, and moderate care protects them from discases, which are seldom dangerous. They sell the wool of the sheep and the skins of the goats to great advantage, and their flesh is their favourite meat; but few horses are kept, because their food is so expensive. Only sheiks and owners of several tents and herds possess them, and employ them in their excursions and in war. I saw no cows beyond Vadi Senetzerk, but it is said that there are some in the camps of Medsched and Dscherar. Of their milk they make a thinnish butter, to which they give an agreeable flavour by mixing it with pounded dates and honey, and preserve it in leather bottles. Asses are every where but few in number, and not very serviceable. Dogs are more numerous and important for guarding the tents and herds: the former against the pilfering Arabs from the caravans that pass by, and the latter against the attacks of the wolves which hide by day in the clefts of the rocks.

Luxuries are not to be thought of among these children of Nature. Every thing is adapted to their situation, and their most pressing wants, simple and uniform, like the country they inhabit. Around their low black tents, which stand in groups, we see nothing but naked children and dogs, who furiously attack the passing stranger, while the women under the tents superintend the domestic concerns. The same plants occur every where, and most of them when slightly agitated fill the air with perfume. Many, formerly common, are perhaps become extinct for want of care, as well as many kinds of animals, though they are less exposed to the pursuit of their most dangerous enemy. It seems as if animals were inspired with greater fury against each other the less they are disturbed by their common foe; and from the little ant, which destroys beetles ten times its own size, to the vulture, eagle, and wolf, all animals of prey follow, without bounds, the instinct which leads them to spread death and destruction around.

Traces and Remains of the Ancient Inhabitants of this Country.

This whole district was once one of the most populous and cultivated in Africa. Alexandria extended nearly as far as Marabut, which is testified by the scattered fragments of marble and granite pillars, walls, and rubbish. The remains of the baths of Cleopatra give indeed a faint idea of its ancient splendour; but a better is supplied by the catacombs, which extend in all directions over a space of nearly half a German square mile, and in whose vicinity there are other tombs hewn in the limestone rock. Near Marabut, on the lake, there are traces of an opulent city, which extended to the plain now overflowed by the lake. On the dam, foundations of towns, formed of large hewn stones, and many cisterns, are to be seen at small intervals. The remains, a quarter of a league from Kareir, are distinguished by their extent; and the foundations on a mountain, four hundred paces from the tower of the Arabs, show that a castle once stood there. On the sea-shore numerous traces of large habitations are met with, among which those near Mizan are the most considerable; and how many may be buried in the Lake Mareotis.

Ruins of Abousir

But the most remarkable are the ruins of the city of Abousir, in the fertile plain and near the well of the same name, twelve leagues from Alexandria on the sea. Three hundred paces from it, situated on an eminence, is the half-ruined monument, called the Tower of the Arabs. The harbour appears to have been only one hundred and forty paces broad, and lies in such a direction, that ships were exposed both to the north and west winds. The same may be said of the other ancient harbours on the coast, between Parætonium and Jaffa, and confirms the observation of Diodorus Siculus, that there was no safe harbour on it except Alexandria. The maritime trade on it could, therefore, be then only carried on in summer. These, as well as the rest, such as Leucaspis, Phœnices, Lygis, and others, are now filled up by sand, and except a few traces entirely vanished. The greater part of the city lay on the southern side of the dam, and was half a league in circumference. Foundations and heaps of rubbish show us the situation of its houses. This rubbish contains pieces of earthen vessels, marble, mosaic, and bricks, the latter particularly of a conical form, of a very beautiful red, and great hardness. Upon the dam no ruins remain, except of the principal building, which I think was a temple. The front western part is nearly entire; of the other three sides only the top part is destroyed. On the west side there are small chambers in three stories, one above the other, and on the same side, in the interior, is a flight of steps, leading into subterraneous apartments, now filled with rubbish. There is also a deep well, and every where substructions. The eastern and western walls are one hundred and thirty-five paces, the northern and southern one hundred and ten paces long. The bricks are fifteen inches long, and nine inches high. In the entrance gallery, sixty paces long and thirty broad, there are also fragments of columns. To the south-west there was a large enclosed space, the pillars of which are still standing, and which I take to have been a garden. It lay low, in a feeble clayey soil, and water was collected in the cisterns close by, against the dry season. Every where, especially on the south side of the mountain, many large and small, for the most part oblong, cisterns and burying places are hewn in the rock; the latter are either deep, with many divisions, or single, but all empty, or at the most with a few mouldered bones, that indicate their original destination. The principal one, under the Tower of the Arabs, appears to be of great extent, and to be connected with it. This tower is doubtless a monument erected in the time of the Ptolemies; octangular below, above round and smaller, constructed of large hewn stones, and the whole belonged to the temple, which was probably dedicated to Osiris. The ruins in this country, from Abousir to Agaba, may be ascribed to three different ages; some are of the times of the Ptolemies or Romans, others of that of the Saracens, and others of the later period of the Arabs. As criteria we may take the structure of the remaining walls, the letters on them, the solidity of the foundations, materials, coins found on the spot, and other circumstances, which are indeed less certain than the appearance of the buildings themselves, but yet, in general, characteristic. It is certain that the later Arabs left the materials in the roughest state, did not measure or cut them by the rule, and in no case prepared marble or bricks for them. The Saracens too seem not to have done the latter; but they were more accurate in fitting the stones, and did not, like the Arabs, content themselves with small stones, but built with large ones, and in a solid manner. The remains of places built in the times the Ptolemies and the Romans have a very different appearance. There we find beautiful red bricks, pieces of white marble, and regular foundations of fine free-stone. Lastly, the proof deduced from coins has some weight. I found a very interesting coin of Alexander the Great about half way between Kasr Dschedebye and Siwa, which was also the high road from Parætonium to that place. The coins found in the rubbish of old towns are worthy of attention. The more we meet with, the more do they confirm the criteria above laid down. We may add the testimony of the in-

habitants, who, though they care little about antiquity, often observed, when they saw a heap of ruins, " This is of the times of
the Greeks, that of the Christians, and this again of the Arabs."

The first ruin we have to mention here is a mosque, called by
the inhabitants *Lamaid.* It is on the sea, six leagues from
Abousir, on the north foot of the chain of hills on which the village (now in ruins) was situated.   Both were built by the Arabs.
There is no trace of any more recent edifice.   An inscription on
the entrance contains some verses from the second Sura of the
Koran; the shape of the letters and the nature of the building
do not allow us to date it further back than the fifteenth century.
Abdermain, four leagues to the west, and two leagues from the
sea, is the ruin of a dwelling.   There are many foundations of
other buildings round it.   The walls are full of Hebrew and
Greek inscriptions of later times.   The solidity and beauty of the
structure induce us to refer it to the time of the Ptolemies.   The
ruins of Kasr Schamaa Garbye, a monument of the age of the
Ptolemies, are two leagues to the west, and three from the sea.
Kasbau Sardsch Scharkyc, twelve leagues more to the west, and
two from the sea, is a handsome monument of the times of the
Ptolemies.   The handsome and very solid structure, and the letters Ω Ψ ע irregularly carved, and dating from the remotest times,
are decisive.   An inscription in these and other strange letters,
which are found here and there, would be highly interesting, but
we could not discover any.   It is hollow within, square, and about
twelve feet high.   The upper part is wanting, and it is difficult to
assign what its destination may have been.   *Kasbau Sardsch
Garbise,* two leagues from the above, one league from the sea,
and half a league from Senetzerk, is the remainder of a large
building.   Its age is decided by the Greek letters cut in many of
the square stones.   Near it, besides the substructions of the
building belonging to this ruin, are many others.   Fifteen paces
south of the ruin is a catacomb, with the entrance on the west
side ; the interior is only five feet long by three feet and a half
broad, with several receptacles for coffins.   Near it is a well (but
without water) and to the west a large palm bush.   I think these
four ruins last mentioned were on the high road to Parætonium:
Kasr Medsched on the sea, near the well of the same name, in a
picturesque country, are the remains of a large fortified building,
which was destroyed only a few years ago by Mahomet Ali
Pacha, and formerly served the Bedouins of these parts as a lurk-
ing place and corn magazine.   There are very fruitful gardens near
it, and a small harbour, in which there were formerly a few ships,
that traded between this place and Alexandria and Derna.   In
ancient times there was probably a sea-port town here.   *Kasr
Rasa Belaha* was a large mis-shapen building on the sea, near the

well of the same name, built by the later Arabs, and probably used as a magazine.   It has several divisions, and the walls are so high, that I think it was also used as a defence against the hordes that passed this way.   Kasr Dschdebye, four leagues from the sea, eighty from Abousir, and four from Agaba, is the largest of all the ruins, but uninteresting as an architectural monument.   It is a parallelogram, sixty-two paces from east to west, and seventy-two from north to south.   There is a small cabinet in each corner. The structure, and some coins found in it, induce me to attribute it to the Saracens.   Near it, especially on the west, there are numerous substructions.   There are many sepulchres of Santons on the plain, and still more on the eminences.   Great respect is paid to these monuments, and no infidel may enter the inner space.   I was often desired to go to a distance from them.   The other Mahometans think in the same manner; in many places I was pursued because I stopped in the burying-grounds.   Once on my reading to an Arab servant the inscription on a sepulchre, he ran away with reverential awe, saying the deceased knew it.

  But what is far more interesting than these shapeless masses of stones, are the foundations and other remains of ancient towns and villages, which I traced whenever circumstances would permit.   The whole tract from Alexandria and Damanhour to the slope of Agaba, and from the sea-coast to the distance of eight or ten leagues, is strewn all over with them.   The group of hills of Elgaibe was far more peopled and fertile than the southern and western plain.   Many cisterns and foundations of villages of the times of the Greeks and the Arabs are scattered here.   The nearer you approach the well of Maddar, the oftener you meet with traces of considerable places, and there certainly was a sea-port town near it.   In the low plain between Maddar and Senetzerk, on the southern elevation, there were several villages, and the fruitful hollows to the north, between the above-mentioned four ancient ruins and the sea, were certainly well inhabited, as is testified by numerous well-built cisterns and fine substructions.   To the north of Senetzerk, on a hill on the sea-shore, the solid foundations of a temple and other edifices, and innumerable pieces of marble and valuable stone, show that an opulent town must once have stood there.   The further you go from the sea the less does the country seem to have been peopled; but even at the distance of ten leagues spots are found with the most luxuriant vegetation, and walls and foundations of buildings.   All these remains indicate a high degree of prosperity, and it would be interesting on that account to determine the geographical situation of the most important places in the Mareotic district mentioned by Ptolemy. The intercourse which is still carried on between the Bedouins of this country and Siwa, was probably very considerable in those ages when the population was so much more numerous. Perhaps in ages anterior to all history, the Lybians dwelt in these fertile tracts on the sea-coast, and kept up from hence a most intimate connexion with the inhabitants of the Oasis of Jupiter Ammon, or partly dwelt there themselves, and whose descendants, Inachus, Phoroneus, Cecrops, and Danaus, made the Greeks acquainted with the worship of Jupiter Ammon, whom we find in such high honour among them. This, however, applies only to the Mareotic district. The other part is better calculated for shepherd tribes. Only on the sea, and on the great road leading by Parætonium into the Pentapolis, it is likely that more numerous tribes resided, in the later times of the Persians and the Ptolemies, to which some of the ruins we have mentioned may be referred.

Of the coins which I found in the ruins of these places, some are of the times of the Saracens, and sufficiently prove that they inhabited all the coasts of this country. But most of them are Greek, or even older, and in a very bad state of preservation. Arabic writers testify that Christians inhabited this tract. Their obstinate resistance against the Mahometans was perhaps the cause of the entire destruction of all the places in which they dwelt. The Sultans of Egypt also bore sway here, till the country became the scene of the wanderings of the Bedouins.

The present Inhabitants of this Country.

The present inhabitants are Bedouins. They live in camps, which they remove from time to time, from two to three hundred families together, under black tents of hair-cloth, which are very spacious, but low, and set up in several rows, each family having one or more, according to its ability. The women hardly ever dwell separately, but form throughout the day a circle apart, without mixing in that of the men. The chief of each camp is a Sheik. The most powerful in this district are Valedali, Dschimeat, and Garbi. They were formerly independent; but for these ten years they have paid to the Pacha of Egypt an annual tribute in kind; for instance, dates, which the Sheik pays for the rest, receiving an indemnity. Their occupation is as simple as their provisions. The women prepare their plain food, keep the tent and domestic economy in order, braid mats, and tend the domestic animals. The men guard the flocks, cultivate the ground, carry their produce for sale to Damanhour, the rendezvous of these Bedouins, Alexandria, or Masr, accompany the camels they have hired out, and, as soldiers born, defend the cause of the Pacha, as they formerly did their own against each other. The horde of Valedali furnishes above 800, Dschimeat 400, Garbi 250 men. Besides many small caravans, we saw one of above a thousand camels,

conducted by these Bedouins, conveying corn, beans, and manufactured goods from Egypt to Barbary, and others returning thither from Derna with wool and skins. This communication is the
more frequent, as the nearer way by Siwa is more inconvenient, and
the voyage by sea along the coast dangerous. Hence there is a
continual traffic backwards and forwards at the three passages
over the high Agaba, near the sea, where they centre. These
Bedouins have lost much of their peculiar character since the
Pacha subdued them, drew their chiefs to his court, and made
them take Damanhour, instead of Meschid, for their rendezvous.
Yet many of them still lead the simple patriarchal life which the
poets have described in such pleasing colours. Their dress is very
simple, and their diet plain, consisting of peas, beans, or barley
flour, mixed with pieces of barley bread and boiled, or bread
baked liked flat cakes, and eaten with onions. Butter is in general
use; only the children take milk; meat is seldom eaten. They
are very fond of dates, which they buy very cheap at Siwa.
They eat every thing from wooden platters, with the hollow hand,
and sitting on the ground. In many camps the boys learn to
read and write, and even the men employ much time in this
manner. They grow up without education, and are generally
very confined in their ideas. Their conversations are seldom instructive, and always very monotonous. I have often observed
them to talk for hours together about single words that one of us
had let fall, without doing any thing but repeat and wonder
at them. They never fish, and seldom hunt, though game is so
abundant. They often take gazelles alive, early in the morning,
while they are asleep. They are bad marksmen with the gun,
and find it more convenient to train falcons for the chace. Thefts
never occur among them, except that the passing caravans often
rob the flocks at pasture, for which reason they are kept at a distance from the usual track of the caravans, and one of the shepherds watches on an eminence to give warning of the approach
of danger. They are little, lean, and sunburnt. Though these
lords of the desert lead such a healthy and peaceful life, they seem
to be subject to many cares, diseases, and even premature death.
They often asked our advice and our medicine, but could never
resolve to pay the two physicians any thing. Some promised to
shew their gratitude, but not unless the medicine did them good.
Some had cauterized the back of the neck, which is said to be a
common mode of cure among the Arabs. Their inattention to time
is so great, that few of them can tell their own age. Mohammed,
Achmed, Achsin, Achfeidha, Aberkau, are common names among
them. In their frequent conversations about us they always distinguished us by some epithet, as, the tall, the short, the rich, &c.
I had taken the name of Ben Jacob. Their remembrance of

places is still more defective than that of names. Though I was often six leagues from the caravan, I always found it again by minding the direction; once I was less fortunate, having gone with two Bedouins and a Hadschi from Tunis to look at the ruins of Kasb Scharkije, which took us a considerable distance from the caravan, and when we attempted to overtake it, the Bedouins missed the way. We luckily met with some shepherds, who directed us to the camp of Medsched. The inhabitants received us well, and listened attentively to our account of the object of our journey. We supped and slept very comfortably on their carpets in the open air, and rejoined the caravan on the following day. They are zealous Mahometans, and, like their brethren, hate and despise infidels, and are inclined to superstition; believers in astrology and charms against diseases; on which subject I found several books among them, one of which had the title of *Ketab Matzchn*. There are few children, and still fewer grown up persons, who have not five or more amulets (or written charms) about their heads and necks. While we stayed at Kasr Dschdebie, they often came to our tent, and were fond of reading in my Arabic books. This was done aloud in a large circle of Bedouins. The reader made remarks on the text, and they all listened for hours together with an attention which surprised me, as the subject was very dry, *e. g.* the Nubian Geography. I became every day a greater favourite with them, and they wished to keep me for some months in their camp. A book written by a Christian, containing dialogues, sentences, and proverbs, interested them still more, and the Sheiks took particular delight in this book, which I unwillingly lent them, because it contained violent attacks on the Mahometans, and I was extremely embarrassed when they read these. Unfortunately our Dragoman came up on this occasion, and laughed, which so vexed the Sheik, that he pelted him with stones. I spoke very seriously, saying that the author was a Christian, and had spoken of them, as many of them do of us Christians. They were satisfied with this explanation, but the Sheik indulged in the most abusive language against the author and the Dragoman. They showed me their whole stock of MSS. One priest had fifteen, all on theological subjects. I obtained some for a copy of the Nubian Geography. They offered to sell me the Koran, and wished much to possess our Gospels. None of our Bedouins performed regularly the five daily prayers, most of them not at all, though many bore the honourable title of Hadschi, or Hadgi. In general I did not observe that the Bedouins were scrupulous in this respect. Only once, when a priest from a neighbouring camp was with us, I saw them all at Mogreb, regularly drawn up, and perform their prayers in the usual form.

Travellers have always spoken with enthusiasm of the hospitality of the Bedouins, and they sometimes certainly received us well, gave us, without interest, water and provisions, and answered for our safety and our property; but in general they made us pay a high price, not only for provisions, but for every little service; coveted every thing they saw; stole even our provisions, which they seemed to consider as common property; and when they meant to behave particularly well, gave us their camel's flesh and barley bread, for our biscuit, rice and mutton, which were ten times as valuable. The Bedouins of this country are, however, not so bad as they were represented to us. As the Sheik was answerable for our lives, we were never to go to a distance from the caravan without his knowledge, and without being accompanied by one of his soldiers. But sometimes the soldier would go his way, and I mine; sometimes he had no mind, and I generally went alone. I was often six leagues from the caravan, saw camps at a distance, had long conversations with Bedouins belonging to them, and nobody ever seemed disposed to do me any violence. On the contrary they gave me water and bread, and smiled at my embarrassment and distrust. On the 4th of November I went from Bir Dokan to the sea, in hopes of finding traces of Parætonium. I met with many who wished to approach me, but I always avoided them, and nobody pursued me. Late in the evening, as I was returning, I met a flock of sheep; the shepherd came towards me, seemingly surprised at my being so late in this solitude. As I avoided him, and walked faster, he called and ran after me; but when I ran as fast as I could he stood still. In our camp they thought I was lost, and sent two of our Bedouins after me, who missed me, and did not return till the next day. The caravans too that I met were very obliging to me, and their observations made me conjecture that the worst Bedouins of the country had been given to us. In the desert they consider themselves as masters, and fear neither the Pacha nor any other. If they were threatened, they threatened in return. If we began to negociate, there was no coming to a conclusion, and if any thing was required of them, they made a thousand objections. They held together when one of them was offended, otherwise they were continually quarrelling with each other.

To our great sorrow we found that even the Bedouins trouble their heads with politics, and tell lies, as in Europe. Thus a caravan passing by, affirmed that the Pacha of Egypt would make war on the Franks, and was already preparing for that purpose. We did our utmost to contradict this report, so dangerous to our safety, and were aided by another piece of news from the neighbouring camps, that the Pacha was certainly preparing for war, not against the Christians, but against the Sultan. Political motives were assigned to our journey to the Cyrenaica. The whole country from Bengasi to Abousir was soon full of the report that we were going, as emissaries of the Pacha of Egypt, into Tripoli, to prepare the way for him to conquer it; also that we were going to fetch treasures which had long been known to us, and for which, according to private accounts, the covetous Bey of Bengasi had resolved beforehand to make us pay dear. Some guessed that conquests were projected by the Franks, as a general was at the head of the caravan. The rapidity with which the report was spread in all directions was evident from the fact, that the Bedouins in Middle Egypt spoke to me on the subject. Even in Syria they talked of it. A report was spread among the Bedouins at the well Chamam, that our caravan had been plundered and murdered in the Tripolitan territory. Several Bedouins had told us already at Kasr Dschdebije that this was intended. Two distant hordes, notorious as robbers, had resolved to surprise us in the night, and only the exaggerated accounts of our double-barrelled guns, and our night watches, had hitherto deterred them. Our Bedouins were much afraid of them, and both on the first and second day after our departure from Siwa, we were obliged to be prepared for an attack. Thus was our caravan in considerable danger among these Bedouins, and it was high time for it to retire on account of the attention that it excited. When, therefore, Otman, the Sheik, who had been with our letters of recommendation to the Bey of Bengasi came back on the 10th of November, he was much displeased at our separation from the general; and when news came that the Bey of Bengasi had indeed received our letters of recommendation, but would first ask the advice of his superior, the Pacha of Tripoli, we were convinced that the expedition was ill arranged, and that the execution of it was impracticable. The answer and the escort, for which we waited, and without which we could not travel in the very dangerous territory of Tripoli, would perhaps never have reached us; a new messenger, if dispatched to Derna and Bengasi, would not have brought the final answer in less than sixty days; which was the shortest time the Bedouins allowed for it.

The language of these Bedouins is the Arabic, but rather corrupted in their pronunciation, like any other language in the mouths of the peasants. As their mode of writing is between that of Egypt and that of Barbary, so is their language also; it may therefore be difficult to find peculiar words among them, but more easily some that have acquired a peculiar signification.

The words of their songs are as indecent as their language; the grimaces and motions with which they accompany the song are as immodest as their conduct when they are alone, and even in company with the other sex. A single verse entertains them for hours together. One sings while dancing ; the others answer by clapping their hands; or he makes while singing all kinds of lasei‑vions, angry or joyful motions, while those around him leap up, but without changing their place. Often he makes those move‑ments with another, who acts the part of a girl, always in quick time, lively and even violent. They generally made a circle in the evening, when two sang and the others danced. Even when tra‑velling they leaped behind, or on the side of the caravan, one sang, and the others answered in chorus. Their leaping most resembles the Cossack dances.

The Country between Agaba and Siwa.

As soon as you have ascended the rising ground of Agaba, you behold on all sides a boundless plain, rich in vegetation, which, like that already described, is inhabited towards the west, but towards the south is quite deserted. The vegetation is also more scanty to the southward, till at length we find only a few insulated verdant spots, after going twelve leagues, very rarely any plants ; and then to Siwa hardly any thing but stony, clayey, or sandy plains and ridges of hills. The beaten track, into which we came on the 15th of November, eight leagues beyond Agaba to the south‑east, is marked by many heaps of stones ; every one of our Bedouins added something to the heaps: an excellent custom in a desert where the way is so seldom to be dis‑covered. It is the great road, which in the remotest times led from these parts, especially from Paraetonium to Siwa. A league further we came to a spot which has always been considered as highly dangerous. The roads from the sea side, Alexandria, Derna, Bengasi, and Augela, meet here. Many caravans are plundered and murdered at this place, and we saw many traces of such. We were obliged to have our guns ready, and the Bedouins, who always magnify the danger to enhance their own importance, kept up a continual firing.

The Oasis is recognized at the distance of four leagues by the great chain of mountains that surround it, and the sight of which excited the greatest joy. The nearer we approached, the more interesting was the prospect. Sometimes they are regularly formed like walls, sometimes pointed, then round, high or low, and quite bare. Lime-stone is predominant. Petrifications, sea‑snails, muscles, oysters, wood, and many large pieces of gypsum, are found every where, all mingled together in the greatest con‑fusion. After winding for half a league between these mountains, and admiring the fine echo, we came, continually descending, into the Oasis itself. These mountains present on the inner side a far more picturesque prospect, and it is surprising how these masses of sand have been able so long to withstand the assaults of the winds and torrents of rain. In the desert between Agabá and Siwa, sandstone is predominant, then quartz and limestone, and the surface is in many places strewed with carnelian and flintstone. This may be said of the whole Lybian desert. The component parts of the boundless plains, chains of hills, or insulated eminences, are sometimes sand, more rarely clay, and sometimes entirely masses of stone. The vegetation is less varied than on the sea-side, and it is singular that we found here in the desert, plants that were quite green, while on the sea-side they were entirely withered.

The race of animals diminishes in the same proportion as the plants. Locusts swarm in the spots where plants are found; and there was also abundance of flies, moths, and lizards. A water-hen, probably from Siwa, had strayed eight leagues south of Agaba. Ravens and other fowls of prey are likewise seen in the neighbourhood. Fifteen leagues further to the south there are probably only ostriches, and hyenas, and these in small numbers.

This desert never was inhabited, on account of the want of water and the barrenness of the soil. In the remotest ages it was crossed from Alexandria, twelve days journey from Siwa, or from the very populous tract on the sea-coast, to fetch the productions of Siwa and Augela, or to proceed thence into the interior of Africa.

Siwa.

The particularly fertile part of the Oasis of Jupiter Ammon, is, according to the inhabitants, one day's journey in circumference, about four leagues long, and from half to three-quarters of a league broad. From east to west it lies very low. On the north side there are many bare mountains, which for about five leagues inclose the hollow, but gradually diminish, and become similar to the high uneven bank which is on the south side of the Oasis. The soil of the plain is throughout sandy, mixed with salt; the sand is on the surface, and the salt a foot deep in great abundance. I did not observe that the earth is covered with salt after rain, though I examined it on the 23d of November, when we had some pretty heavy showers. The mountains, which are from 200 to 500 feet high, consist of sand or limestone. The Oasis is strewed with the above-mentioned petrifications, especially near to the eminences on the south and north sides. Salt lakes are in the east part, another in the west part of the Oasis. Streams flow through it in all directions, and run into the little lakes. Twenty springs of fresh water, (among which is the fountain of the Sun near the Temple,) almost as many of brackish water, and frequent rains in the two winter months, fertilize the soil. Meadows, bushes, palm-groves, gardens, and corn-fields, diversify the scene, and the most luxuriant vegetation delights the eye. The lakes are covered with water-fowl; in the gardens there are palms, olives, pomegranates, plums, vines, melons, &c. The dates, which are far better than those of Angela, and esteemed equal even to those of Tunis, are annually exported in great quantities to Alexandria and Cairo. The pomegranates are excellent, and remarkably large. Barley, rice, and beans, are cultivated in the fields.

In the animal world the varieties are as few as in the vegetable kingdom, but equally numerous. Worms, insects, (especially flies, lice, and fleas,) are found every where; and domestic animals, such as cows, asses, goats, sheep, dogs, cats, fowls, &c. are very numerous. Camels cannot live here, and in some years, many of those belonging to the caravans die from the effects of the plants, and the water of this country. It is necessary to feed them with dates, and to give them water very rarely. Even this does not save them at certain seasons of the year. The inhabitants are also very numerous, though uncivilized. The number of the men is said to be above 3000. Thus, in a small spot in the midst of the desert, where, for the distance of six to twelve days journey round scarcely a living being is to be seen, there reigns a degree of animation, such as may be sought in vain in the most fertile parts of Europe, and which fully confirms all that Diodorus, Arrian and Curtius, have said of the fertility of this Oasis.

Hence, it was always, and in the remotest ages, very well peopled, and we every where found traces of more flourishing times. The ruins of the temple of Jupiter Ammon (now called Haima Caida,) are the most important, and most renowned. M. Drovetti possesses a very accurate drawing of them. Of the three parts of which, according to Strabo, this temple consisted, only two can now be distinguished in the space where the ruins lie. The foundations of the third division are probably under the adjacent houses. The people told us of the remains of seven towns, and particularly of a Heathen and of a Christian city. The Catacombs on the mountain *El Messagaret,* which the inhabitants believe to be of the highest antiquity, and where accurate researches would probably lead to many interesting discoveries; those on Mount *Rakije* and others, and the ruins of Busruf, Korascha, Otbeija, and Lawaw, on the eastern parts of the Oasis, bear testimony to this fact. These remains likewise inform us who were the earlier inhabitants. The architecture, the paintings and hieroglyphics, indicate the most remote antiquity, and their derivation from the Egyptians, whose usual works of art they surpass by the superior correctness of their forms. It is unanimously asserted that several statues have been used in the foundations of houses, but they are sought in vain among the ruins. It is probable that the number of them was never considerable, on account of the distance of the materials. But we have more reason to be surprised that no ancient coins are now to be found on this spot, where such rich offerings were made to Jupiter Ammon, for a happy journey, by the caravans going into the interior of Africa. After repeated inquiries, and after search made by many of the inhabitants, one of them at length brought me a piece of small money coined at Malta in 1760, which he declared to be the oldest coin to be found in Siwa. Most of the other ruins are probably of later date. The earlier inhabitants, like the present, had doubtless some intercourse with those of the Mareotic territory, and with them adopted Christianity in the second century. Several bishops of this Oasis are mentioned in the history of the Patriarchs of Alexandria. Mahometanism spread there in the seventh century. After the depopulation of the Mareotic district, they attained an independence, in which, according to the testimony of Arabian writers, they have seldom been disturbed, and which they still endeavour to maintain, though they have been obliged, for these six years past, to pay tribute to the Pacha of Egypt.

The present inhabitants of Siwa live in four miserable villages, built in the Arabian manner, which are placed upon eminences, and surrounded with high walls to protect them from hostile attacks. Below Siwa Kebir (the principal place) there is towards the north, an enclosed space, which is generally occupied in winter by the caravans; with a small mosque in it, dedicated to Sheik Soleiman, and close to it three large date magazines, called by them Masdack, where they keep and expose to sale their whole stock. They sort the dates very carefully, and give each kind a different name. Their annual produce is so large that 500 camel loads are exported. We were allowed to eat as much as we pleased, without payment; the only proof of hospitality that we received during our stay. They carry on their trade by barter, exchanging their dates, olives, cattle, and handsome baskets made of palm leaves, for corn, tobacco, manufactured goods, especially linen, coffee, &c., which are brought by the Arabs from Alexandria, or by the Bedouins. They are much attached to the Mahometan law, and hate more or less all who are not of their religion. We experienced the effects of this hatred; none of their Sheiks visited us in our tents, and our interpreter was always obliged to wait at the door of the house, for the permission which we often asked, but in vain, to visit the curiosities of the Oasis.

There are several Sheiks, over whom a governor is placed by the Pacha. The majority of the inhabitants consist of natives; but there are likewise many negroes from the interior of Africa, sixty or eighty days'. journey distant. This mixture had some influence on their manners and language. They live on very plain food, chiefly their own produce, and their distress differs but little from that of the inhabitants of Egypt. They have not a healthy look, and are said seldom to live to a great age. Almost every year many are carried off by a fever, caused by the water and unripe fruit, which is said to be often contagious. Their complexion is dark; their physiognomy between that of the Egyptians and the negroes, and of a middle stature. They are selfish, but yet good-natured, and the ill treatment and hindrances we experienced are not to be ascribed to them, but to their Sheiks and Imans, and our Bedouins, who lusted after our presents, which were intended for the principal people at Bengasi and Derna. Our Bedouins desired many of them to beat us: they replied we were under the special protection of the Pacha, to which the malicious Bedouins returned that the Pacha was at a distance; but they said we were good people and had not offended them; why then should they beat us?

. Their language is different from the Arabic, which they, however, both speak and write, and in this manner they may have become assimilated. Their pronunciation is more guttural than that of the Arabs, and our Bedouins assured me that they had much difficulty in understanding them when they conversed among themselves. An accurate knowledge of all the words in this langnage, which are not Arabic, will prove that it is identical with the Schillah, which is spoken by many tribes of northern Africa, and contains many words from the Punic, from which it has probably been formed.

. In giving these short notices, I must beg the reader to consider the painful situation of our party. I was always prepared, to risk even my life, to converse freely with the inhabitants, and to visit their curiosities, but the danger to which I should thereby expose my companions, obliged me to do the first privately, and silently to refrain from the latter. It was only on our departure that I separated from them, without, however, obtaining much more than a general local knowledge, for we could not find the Temple, and the fountain of the Sun, and none of the inhabitants would show us the way. We ascended several eminences, and found the above statements of the inhabitants respecting the extent of the Oasis in general confirmed. Though this Oasis is separated from the tract on the sea-coast by an extensive desert, the climate is nearly the same, the numerous lakes, streams, and springs, having the same effect as the vicinity of the sea.

This Oasis was formerly notorious for the robberies committed on travellers. Our Bedouins, most of whom had been before, pointed out the places where the banditti lay in ambush, and we always had to put ourselves in a posture of defence in their neighbourhood. But the cannon of the Pacha of Egypt has spread terror among them, and they not only pay him a regular annual tribute in dates, but seldom attack caravans travelling under his protection. To me, however, the inhabitants appear less suspicious than the vagabonds who resort hither from all parts of northern Africa, and return home with their booty along with the caravans.

Description of the Country between Siwa and Kara.

The two chains running to the east, which enclose Siwa, go for eight leagues nearly parallel in this direction. Four leagues beyond the Oasis the ground is less salt, and the vegetation more scanty. Sometimes you see tufts of shrubs, and on the right, at a distance, a grove of palms. The mountains are in the greatest disorder, and the whole tract has the appearance of having been once the bed of a great salt lake, which was the deepest where Siwa now is, in which the slime collected with all kinds of fertilizing substances; it seems to have been from one to two and a half leagues in breadth, through an extent of seven and a half leagues from east to west, to have then divided into the south-western and north-eastern arms, to have contained several small islands, its being sandy and its banks of limestone. The bed of the south-eastern arm declines twenty leagues east of Siwa into another little Oasis, called Kara, and also *little Siwa*. The windings, which this hollow makes eight leagues beyond Siwa, oblige the caravans to leave it. We come into a boundless desert plain, where for eight leagues together we see nothing but some bare hills, and tracks of caravans. Then follow fresh strata of limestone, and hollows, furrowed and undermined by torrents of rain. The Arabs call this place Regebel Bagle. You cannot proceed a step here without meeting with petrifications. Petrified fungi were particularly numerous. Sand hills stand close to strata of limestone of manifold forms, striped with black, red, and yellow, the confirmation of which indicates some great revolution.

Kara extends three leagues in length from north-east to south-west, and is half a league in breadth. It has five springs of fresh water, of which that in the well of Kara, at the foot of the mountain on which the village stands, is remarkably good. The vegetation is not so luxuriant as in Siwa, the shrubs, trees, and animals, fewer, and the population very small, the men being only forty in number. In religion, language, and manners, they resemble those of Siwa; they know nothing of any ruins of ancient edifices. They are very poor, live in half ruined houses, and pay little attention to the cultivation of their gardens, and their only crops are barley and dates. Since the visit of the Pacha many of the inhabitants have removed to Siwa or Masr.

Description of the Country between Kara and Libbuk.

As soon as we leave the hollow of Kara, we see to the right and left naked mountains, and to the left in particular, a chain extending from west to east to the vicinity of Terraneh, and connected with the above-mentioned hollow or dell. We proceeded either along the foot of them, or a quarter or half a league off, till one league from Libbuk. On this journey the most fertile spots were at Cheische, eleven leagues from Kara, and at Bomarsu, three leagues further, about half way between Kara and Libbuk. This last is a plain about two leagues long, and half a league broad, where the vegetation is very rich, with some palms, and a well, the water of which even the animals will not drink. The summit of the chain is from 200 to 400 feet above the supposed bed of the lake, which is connected with the Oasis. It goes sometimes to the north-east, and sometimes to the south-east, but seldom due east, yet we chiefly kept close along the chain of mountains where the track of the caravan is, because the Bedouins assured us that there were dangerous holes under the stratifications, which lie piled upon one another like immense flakes of ice. We saw every where the footsteps of hyenas and wolves, the holes of mice and insects, and a great number of snails. But even the fertile spots of Chiesche, Bomarsu, and Libbuk, seem never to have been the abode of man.

The above-mentioned petrifications, which are also spoken of by Strabo, (p. 49, 50. Edit. Casaub.) are met with in this whole tract; and behind Libbuk there are besides many pieces of petrified palm-trees, black and very solid, which are frequently used as marks to show the way; they are often very large, and their original form is but little altered. Fungi, testaceous limestone, sand, and clay, are the component parts of this whole country, which are observed mixed and confusedly thrown together by storms, but frequently, too, separated in large masses. They often stand alone in the form of a pyramid, and then the various component parts may be easily distinguished, especially the ferragenous parts, which alternating in black, yellow, brown, red, or variegated stripes, make an interesting appearance, but are so friable, that we cannot sufficiently wonder at their long preservation. This lake extended thus far, and perhaps even to the neigh-

bourhood of Terraneh; it varied in breadth and depth, and was
inhabited by all kinds of marine animals. A hurricane, or some
convulsion of nature, broke through the sandy bank, the greater
part of the water of the lake flowed through the plain, which
declines towards the sea, the rest settled in the deep places, where
it fertilized the ground in an extraordinary degree, and made
those beautiful valleys which we call Oases, or where palms and
many trees grow together without needing the hand of man.   It
might now be difficult to fix the point where the waters broke
through.   I should guess two places, where I chiefly observed
the gradual descent towards the sea.   One is north of Siwa,
the second north-east of Kara; the last of which turns to the
east, and then to the north.   There is no point between Libbuk
and Terraneh, where the breach can be supposed to have taken
place.   Our supposition explains the whole nature of this country.   Springs of fresh water, as at Siwa, Kara, Cheische, &c.
are frequently observed in the sea, and in salt lakes.   Whether
the vegetation was first produced by the care of man, or what is
most probable, the seeds were brought thither by the waters
from Egypt, its luxuriance can be explained only by this hypo-
thesis.

Alexandria.

Alexandria lies on a slip of land between the Mediterranean
and Lake Mareotis, in an uncultivated plain, broken by hills only
towards the south, on two large harbours, the old one towards
the west, and the new one towards the north.   Though the soil
seems sandy and sterile, yet in the gardens, and even here and
there in the open country, besides palms, sycamores, and other
trees, many vegetables are cultivated.   Sycamores are seldom
seen here, except in gardens, and they would have become very
scarce in Egypt, had not the present Pacha thought fit to
encourage the cultivation of them, for the sake of the silk worms.
In the Bey's garden there are two apple-trees, and in that of the
English Consul one called Nibga, the fruit of which is the size of
a walnut.   Provisions of almost every kind are procured from
the islands, and Egypt, except poultry, of which there is abundance.   The flies and gnats are very troublesome here, as they
are all over Egypt: but there is no instance of any persons being
mortally wounded by a snake or scorpion.   Many of the inhabitants know how to catch venomous serpents, and teach them to
dance, &c., which is done by stunning them.   All other accounts
of the matter are groundless.   The air is pure, and never too
warm; the nights here and on the whole coast are the heaviest in
June and July.   About this time, and even in April and May,

·the most clouds are seen, but they do not then, any more than in August and September, descend in rain. On the whole coast it rains only in October, November, December, and January, sometimes, but very seldom, in December and February, generally with a south-west wind, seldom with west or north, and never with east or south winds. Of late years there have been two earthquakes in Egypt; one in 1809, the other in 1813; both very violent; the last extended to the whole island of Candia, Lower Egypt, and even a part of Middle Egypt, but neither Alexandria nor Cairo suffered any injury. In general earthquakes were never so dangerous in Egypt as in Asia Minor, the Morea, Sicily, Portugal, and other countries.

Alexandria is full of rubbish of ancient buildings, among which are large pieces of beautiful marble and granite, and many foundations, vaults, and pieces of walls, which are carefully sought after by the Arabs, to be used in new buildings. It is probable that very interesting discoveries are often made, but very little attention is paid to them. Thus, I was told, about thirty-five years ago, many rolls of papyrus were found, but were immediately burned by order of the Bey. I attempted in several places to advise the Arabs who were digging, and direct them to certain objects, but they pelted me with stones. The eastern part of the Pharos, the ancient promontory of Lochius, are under water; the traces of the Circus and the Hippodrome are extremely insignificant; and those of the great palaces of the Ptolemies, their library and baths, have entirely disappeared. They lay on the new harbour, and their foundations might certainly be traced by digging. In the same manner, as the retiring of the sea shewed the halls of Cicero's villa, with their marble seats, at Mola, and as the remains of Regina Diocla have been observed in the water near Perasto, in the Bocche di Cattaro, so have splendid remains of the above-mentioned buildings been seen here under similar circumstances, and not a year passes but stones of inestimable value, and gold and silver coins, are found on the shore.

The baths of Cleopàtra are generally known; the celebrated Scrapium lies to the south-west, near Pompey's Pillar, now out of the city walls. On ascending an eminence you can still plainly see, amidst the rubbish, the wall as it most probably stood; but it is impossible to distinguish the remarkable colonnade, nor is there any trace of the columns of red marble, of which there were sixteen on each of the longer, and sixty-seven on each of the shorter sides. The best proof that the Scrapium stood here, seems, however, to be the discovery made some years since, two hundred and fifty paces south of Pompey's Pillar, when the workmen employed in digging the new canal found several statues erected in honour

of the God of Health, and which are now in the inestimable collection of M. Drovetti.

The foundation of Pompey's Pillar is composed of large pieces
of granite, now repaired with bricks, and cemented with lime.
The pedestal is a single block of granite, the breadth of which
is the same on all sides, namely, five feet eight inches. An
ancient drawing, which is in the house of a Maronite Bishop, on
Mount Lebanon, shews that there was once a statue of bronze on
the pillar, which was coined into money under the Caliphate of
Valid, son of Abdalmalich. A statue of colossal size stands on
the summit; but the drawing is not of such a nature as to enable
us to give any particulars, except that the position of the hands
seem to indicate that they held something. It is not only among
the rubbish that many marble and granite pillars are seen, but in
most of the houses in the city, where they are used for the colon-
nades round the court-yards, for door-posts, &c. Many of the
mosques were once handsome Christian churches, with three aisles,
in a good style, but they are disfigured by changes and decorations
in a bad taste. Of the great church of St. Athanasius only three
fine granite columns now remain. It was converted into a mosque,
which was entirely destro.,ed by the French at the end of the last
century. The church of the Greeks is very old, on the scite of
a prison, where Diocletian caused many Christians to be put to
death. On the ruins of a prison St. Saba built a church, but the
relics were preserved in the patriarchal church at Cairo. Like
the city it has been several times destroyed, and is composed of
all kinds of fragments. It has three aisles, is very small, in the
usual Greek form, with bad paintings, and some statues. In the
chapel of St. Catharine they preserve as a relic the stone with
which martyrdom was inflicted on that saint. Only five monks
live in the convent connected with it, and only sixty men of Alexandria, chiefly merchants, belong to that church. Near it is the
wretched Coptic convent, with a small church, for the very inconsiderable Coptic congregation, which has been lately rebuilt,
having been wholly destroyed during the French invasion. The
Latins have the largest church, and the annexed convent, with
two Franciscan monks from the Holy Land, has gained in extent
and in internal solidity since the present pacha has governed
Egypt. Their congregation generally exceeds two thousand.
The Catholics of the Greek-Armenian persuasion, and also the
Maronites, frequent this church, for want of one of their own;
and they have usually two clergymen here, who are at the same
time schoolmasters. The Latins have not yet established a school,
and prefer sending their children to Europe for education. The
majority of the Franks here never attend the church, and their
morals, as in most of the commercial towns, are greatly corrupted.

The Franks of the Reformed Church baptize and bury in the Greek church. Within these few years both the Latin and Greek convents have hospitals attached to them, (that of the Latins for sixty persons), the object of which cannot be sufficiently commended in a country where the poor stranger is destitute of all assistance and medical advice, and is left to perish, like the natives, who are in general wholly neglected.

Both the interior and the exterior walls of the city were built by the present pacha, but they are not at all adapted to repel a hostile attack. I never saw soldiers on guard so careless as those in the three gates and in the fort. The streets are narrow, crooked, and unpaved; the houses mean, having, instead of windows, wooden lattices, which are often very ingeniously made. Most of the houses have a projection, which contains the apartments of the family. They are seldom painted; when they are it is with landscapes, in which camels are never omitted. In the hope of finding some inscriptions, I examined, but in vain, most of the cisterns in and near Alexandria. They differ little in their construction, but their size is very various. The walls of fifty that I saw were as fresh as if they had been built only a few years ago, and they were in such a rude Arabian style, that there was probably never any intention of adorning them with inscriptions. There is certainly not a single ancient one among them. In the month of September they were almost all without water. It is said there are one hundred of them in and near Alexandria.

The population of Alexandria amounts to 12,000 or 15,000 souls. The Franks live on very good terms with the Mahometans, both here and in the rest of Egypt, and disputes between them are speedily arranged to the satisfaction of both parties, by a commission appointed for the purpose. Trade here becomes active and convenient since the completion of the canal, and the building of the corn magazines. The Franks in Egypt and Syria generally make use of the Italian language, as they do of the French at Smyrna and Constantinople. Their European goods are very dear, for they generally require 400 per cent. profit. There are very few learned Hellenists to be met with here, and it is equally difficult to find among the Mahometans any who have a taste for literature. When I enquired for books, I was always referred to Cairo. The Franks are employed almost exclusively in trade. They live in a very insulated manner; and the dread of the plague confines them to their apartments for the greater part of the year.

Egypt under Mehemet Ali Pacha.

Mehemet Ali Pacha, the present viceroy of Egypt, by his successful expedition against the Wechabites, and another to Nubia, by the establishment of manufactories, by the construction of the canal from Alexandria to Fum el Machmudije, where it joins the Nile, and especially by his commercial connections in all the great maritime cities of Europe, his riches, his respectable military and naval force, and his good treatment of the Franks, has acquired a great and solid reputation. Many of his endeavours to civilize Egypt and to extend her manufactories have indeed failed, because the natives are not fit for such employment, and the Franks require such high wages that his goods cost twice as much as those brought from Europe; but still the endeavour is worthy of praise. The chief obstacle to the improvement of the country, under his government, is the despotism which characterises all his enterprises. He is unlimited master of the soil and all that it produces: nobody has any landed property, and nobody is rich except himself and some of his officers, as long as he permits them to be so. He has the monopoly of the produce of Egypt, and even of the East India goods that come through that country; he suffers no competitors except the few commercial houses whom he favours; and hitherto nobody has been able to resist this despotism. He fixes the prices, treats all merchants and captains of merchantmen at his pleasure, and sells only to his favourites, so that many vessels must leave Alexandria without cargoes, and many merchants have been without any business for some years. If there were not such conflicting interests, the consuls would long since have made complaints to their respective ministers at Constantinople, who would have claimed the execution of the existing commercial treaties. But single complaints make no impression, and the Divan too seems unable to protest with effect against the proceedings of the powerful Pacha. Hence the many merchants who in 1815 and 1816 were at the height of prosperity, but were ruined by misfortunes in 1817 and 1818, will be long involved in distress and never be able to pay the millions of debt to the Pacha. I am assured that within a short period twenty-seven have failed, seven are in imminent danger, and five must give up their business in a few years. In 1820 the Pacha commanded those who could not pay the third part of their debt to him to leave the country. He governs with unlimited power from the Mediterranean to Dongola; from Arish, the Deserts of Arabia, the Red Sea as far as Agaba, Siwah, the Natron territory, the great and little Oases, and even the princes of Sennaar and Darfour now tremble before his mighty arm.

The Bedouins of the Mareotic and Natron territory are his soldiers. The corps of Mamelukes is supplied with recruits from all parts of the Turkish empire, and what his troops want in discipline and skill, is made up by their courage, and the valour of their leaders, and the deficiency of his enemies in cannon and ammunition. About three millions of men are subject or tributary to him, and all Mahometans are answerable for the security of the caravans going in pilgrimage to Mecca. The form of government is well known, and the great influence of some intelligent Franks in the ameliorations that are attempted excite hopes of a real improvement in the state of Egypt. But the most judicious persons entertain doubts on this head, if the Pacha continues to exercise the same tyranny over agriculture and commerce, and the lives of his subjects. Egypt is, besides, deficient in population, which alone can save the Delta, once the most fertile country in the world, from being converted into a desert. The Rosetta mouth of the Nile is so choked up with sand that even small vessels often run aground. They cannot proceed without a strong favourable wind, for which they often have to wait for weeks together. What would become of the Paradise of Egypt; what would become of Rosetta, with its lofty pleasant houses, its fine gardens, its palm groves, and luxurious cornfields, without the overflowing of the Nile? It is to be feared that the masses of sand pressing from east to west, which in the desert between Damietta and Rosetta cover or swallow up like floods of water, lofty pillars, houses, and even palm trees, will soon change into a desert this fine tract, watered by the western arm of the Nile, and the canals that are supplied from it, and will leave only one remaining of the seven arms of the Nile which once fertilized the Delta. Wo to the rulers who for above these thousand years, have contributed by their neglect to bring about so unhappy a result. - The evil cannot be remedied except by a judicious direction of the water upon scientific principles; but numerous hands are requisite to such a work.

Mehemet Ali receives with kindness, fugitives from all parts of the world, and gives them land to cultivate; thus he was a considerable gainer in particular by the late persecutions of the Catholic Greeks in Damascus, and of the Catholic Armenians in Aleppo and Constantinople. The object of his late expedition to Nubia, was also, to obtain an encrease of population for Egypt. But what is gained by these means is lost again by the plague, dysentery, and mortality among children. The most destructive of all evils is the plague, which in the years 1820 and 1821, desolated Alexandria and Cairo, and even committed ravages on board the European vessels to an extent hitherto unknown. It is the more formidable, as both the causes and the remedies against it are unknown. It is certain that it is propagated by contact, but why some persons are more or less susceptible than others of taking the infection, must remain a riddle till physiology is placed on a more steady foundation: it is certainly not a disease of the nerves. It is remarkable that the symptoms partly agree with those pointed out by Thucydides in his account of the contagion at Athens during the Peloponnesian war. The same evil which then afflicted Athens, and now depopulates the Turkish empire, probably raged among the Greeks before Troy. It is therefore old, perhaps as old as the Deluge. Suppose that the typhus had proceeded from the exhalation of the heaps of animal bodies, which must have been dissolved in corruption at that time, and under certain circumstances had been after a lapse of years again developed by contact? Certain periodical winds, such as the chamise in Egypt, and the mode of living among the Arabs, may have an influence, yet the main cause is contact; and therefore a medical police and strict quarantine ought to be introduced, and every thing not left to blind chance. I could adduce many instances of the unhappy consequences of their absurd notions in this respect. At Cairo, an Arab, attempting to save a fowl which had fallen into the river, swam too far from the shore and was carried away by the current. He might easily have been saved by throwing him a rope or an oar; but nothing was done; the Mahometans, of whom great numbers were on the banks and in the vessels, assured me he had been predestined from his birth to perish in this manner. At Alexandria they believe that the plague is brought thither by pilgrims from Barbary and afterwards from that city to Rosetta and Cairo. It generally appears in Alexandria in the month of December and continues, but generally with interruptions, till June. At Cairo it usually commences in March. This periodical recurrence seems to prove the influence of the chamise, which blows with the greatest violence about this time. Some years ago the Pacha wished to introduce a quarantine, but he was induced to renounce his intention, partly by his own commercial interest, and partly by remonstrances which were sent him from Constantinople.

Description of the Country between Alexandria and Cairo.

Ten minutes walk from the exterior south gate of Alexandria is the canal, on which labourers are still employed by command of the Pacha, and corn magazines building at the extreme end of it. Here is the place where all goods to and from Cairo are loaded and unloaded, and also the custom-house. The Arabs are here employed the whole day in loading and unloading the ships and camels. All the trade between Alexandria and Cairo is carried on by this canal, and its importance is greatly enhanced by the increasing danger and difficulty of the navigation at the mouth of the Nile at Rosetta. It is about ten paces broad and twelve leagues long. The southern dam separates it, for the extent of four leagues, from Lake Mareotis, and thence from the fertile plain on which Damanhour lies; the northern dam divides it from the low plain which bounds the sea, and afterwards Lake Madie. In the vicinity of Alexandria there are only huts of the Bedouins on this neck of land, but five leagues distant are considerable villages, such as Elouak and Birket; thither the people of Alexandria often go to shoot qnails and pigeons. There are but few plants on the two banks; but the nearer you approach to Fum el Machmudie, the more interesting does the country become, and in sailing up the Nile the prospect is beyond conception striking and delightful. Towns rapidly succeeding each other, the richest vegetation, groves of palms mingled with corn fields and gardens, where the wonderful productive power of nature makes up for the deficiency of human hands; where earth and water swarm with animal life, and the sky is frequently darkened by the immense flocks of pigeons. The navigation in the canals is less agreeable. Every moment you see the wheels that raise the water into the ditches; every where the painful labour of man is visible, and the less flourishing vegetation and smaller number of towns, render the scene more uniform. One of the most interesting parts, is that where the Nile divides into the two principal branches. Its course is there more rapid, its banks further from each other, and more diversified, and the pyramids are already visible at a distance. The Fellahs in the Delta are good tempered, but most zealous Mahometans. A Neapolitan lately beat one of them severely, because he and some others had been called by an opprobrious name, and thrown stones at some European ladies, whose necks and faces were uncovered. The others were immediately going to murder him, but on his giving money to him that he had beaten, and embracing him, all was made up. Crocodiles are very rarely seen in the Delta, it is only in years when the Nile is very high that one is sometimes seen at Raschid, at which place one of extraordinary size was observed three years ago.

Cairo, and the Christians in Egypt.

The entrance into the capital of Egypt, resembles that into an European city in which there is a much frequented fair. There is a constant throng of people going to and from the adjacent country; the streets are always crowded, and the Bazars, filled with goods of every description, present a very animated and interesting scene. Every moment you have to step aside to avoid being galloped over by the horses or asses, or to force your way through a dense mass of people.

As soon as your effects are landed and inspected by the custom-house officers, a crowd of Arabs fight to get possession of them; each endeavours to load them on his ass, and you are happy to get out of the throng and agree with them at some distance, on the best terms you can.

The population of Cairo is composed of very different parts; Arabs, Turks, Mamelukes, Berbers, Negroes, Jews, Copts, Greeks, Armenians, and Franks, are mingled together, and the temporary residence of the Bedouins and strangers from the interior of Asia and Africa, contribute to diversify the scene. The number of the Franks is small in comparison with the others, and it is only within these few years that they have become so numerous as they now are. There are about fifteen hundred in Cairo, mostly Italian merchants and manufacturers. Most of them have lost their credit by unfortunate speculations, and their business by the tyranny of the pacha. They live in the quarter called Dschamea, enjoy unbounded liberty, and are more esteemed than in any other province of the Turkish empire. There are two Latin convents, each with an ill built and small church: the largest, *Di Terra Santa*, under the protection of the French, as well as those of Alexandria; and Rosetta is under the superior at Jerusalem, in union with those in Palestine, Syria, and Cyprus. The smaller one, of the propaganda, under Austrian protection, is immediately connected with the propaganda at Rome, as well as the convents of Achmin, Tachta, &c. in Upper Egypt. At Cairo there are two priests in each, in the others only one; and at Rosetta and Damietta, for want of Franciscans, their place is supplied by Maronites. In the church of the larger convent, the Maronites and catholic Syrians also celebrate divine worship, and in that of the smaller, the catholic Greeks, Armenians, and Copts. Each of these communities has a vicar-general, and the first has a bishop on Mount Lebanon. Some years ago, the Copts, at the intercession of the pious, wealthy, and very much esteemed Moallem Galli, minister of the pacha, endeavoured to have the worthy vicar-general, Matthias Raschit, consecrated bishop, and had paid large sums to obtain permission. But the malicious schismatics found means, by paying still larger sums to the pacha, to assert, as the predominant church, the right which had been insured to them for some centuries by the sultan, not to permit any catholic bishop, and when the pious old man was going to embark at Damietta to get himself consecrated on Mount Lebanon, they caused him to be so cruelly beaten, that he was ill for several months, became averse to society, and lost many of his admirable qualities. Moallem Galli, who was very ill-treated on this occasion, has since recovered the pacha's favour ; and when the bishop of Babylon, Pietro Couperi, on his way to Bagdad, visited Cairo, there wanted nothing but a worthy priest approved by Rome, for the pacha had now given his permission, out of respect for the presence of the French consul.

This community is the most numerous among the oriental catholics, though it was always the most persecuted by the schismatic Copts. Commercial interest and persecution in Syria have brought the others hither. The Armenians are merchants, and were never numerous. The Greeks in Cairo are about three thousand, Alexandria one hundred, Damietta and Rosetta eighty. The patriarch of Alexandria has his residence in a convent in the Greek street. I frequently saw the intelligent patriarch Theophilus, at Patmos, where he had lived in retirement for these three years.

Their largest and handsomest church is that of St. Nicholas. That of St. Catherine, in the convent of the monks of Mount Sinai, is small but rich, as well as the convent. The convent of St. George in Old Cairo, is remarkable as being erected upon a large handsome ancient building. The language of the church is the Greek, though many are unacquainted with it.

The original inhabitants of Egypt, the Copts, have been reduced by the cruel oppression of the several rulers of the country, and by the plague, to twenty thousand men, or eighty thousand souls in all ; and their churches to one hundred, twenty-three of which, with six convents, are at Cairo. They dwell together in a quarter of Cairo near the patriarch, where there is a handsome new church. They constitute a great part of the population of Old Cairo, where they have several convents which, however, are poor, and inhabited by a very few persons.

Their manners and customs have become assimilated to those of their tyrannical oppressors, with whom they are every where intermixed. Three villages only, in Upper Egypt, have remained unmixed. We seek in vain, especially among the inhabitants of Lower and Middle Egypt, for peculiarities in their religious or domestic customs, their proverbs, way of life, and language. For several years past they have even ceased to celebrate their family festivals at New Year, Epiphany, Easter, and in September, when they dwelt in tents at a distance from their houses, in a temporary oblivion of domestic cares ; when the heads of families treated their relations with the best that their stores could afford, made presents of sweetmeats to the children, especially at Epiphany, and indulged in harmless pleasures. Poverty has deprived them of the means, and tyranny of courage. Only they still celebrate, in social circles, the eighth day after a christening, and the marriage, to which the bride never brings any dowry.

They are remarkable for their good temper, and for a laudable complaisance in the ordinary intercourse of life. Their mode of salutation is very formal and long, always pressing the hand on the breast, then laying it on the hand of the other, and lastly on the head. Perhaps it would be difficult to find a Christian sect which is so degraded, or in which the moral dignity of man is so much effaced. To form an idea of it, we need but go into the churches, and see how the bishops, and still more, the priests, with the stick in their hands, strike the believers who press around like a flock of sheep, and who know of no duties at church but that of mechanically imitating some motion made by the priest.

According to the unanimous assurance of the Coptic patriarchs, and of many monks from Upper Egypt, they have, in their convents, none but new MSS. for the use of the churches, which they read fluently, but do not understand without the help of the Arabic translation opposite. Very few monks in Upper Egypt understand Coptic well, and the patriarch said he had known but one who spoke it. I do not believe that there are any ancient MSS. in the convents, or that the inscriptions in their churches are at all interesting, either to history or paleography. These latter are all new, or repaired, and contain nothing but doxologies in the Coptic language, sentences from scripture, and the names of the saints, who also are badly painted over them in the oriental style. Their patriarch Abga Petrus, shewed me, as the oldest and most valuable article in his little library, a Lectionarium, with the Arabic translation opposite, of the year 1161.

The Coptic literature has certainly to expect the most important acquisitions from the excavations, and from the collections already made, in particular that of the celebrated and excellent M. Drovetti, who possesses, among others, eight partly decayed MSS. containing the Bible in the Saitic dialect, and the Wisdom of Solomon in the Memphitic dialect, which are probably older than any in Europe. He has likewise a fine collection of historical inscriptions. It is only to be lamented that he who is at the expence of making excavations in Egypt, is disappointed by intrigues of the fruit of his researches. The Arabs are bribed, and generally carry off the most valuable of the articles that are found.

The Jews in Africa, the Slaves, and the Gypsies.

The Jews are as much strangers here as in other countries, where they ebb and flow according as commercial speculation, or favour shown them, may determine. The latter, however, seems never to have been the case in Egypt. What political catastrophes have destroyed here, was never restored ; many villages which a few centuries ago belonged to them exclusively, are still desolate, many towns which formerly prospered through their industry, are now decayed, and the few remains of them in Cairo and Alexandria are poor, or new comers from the land of the Franks. Their ancient prosperity is attested by the ruins of many synagogues, particularly in Lower Egypt, and two of them are still held in great honour by all the Jews, on account of a legend, which affirms that one of them possesses a 'Hebrew copy of the Bible, written by Esdras himself, and the other one that was brought to it a thousand years ago in a supernatural manner, as the chapel of the Virgin at Loretto was borne through the air by angels. That the latter was honoured three hundred years ago, is proved by a signature, by which all persons who shall touch this book are excommunicated. What may be said of the Oriental Jews in general is applicable to those of Egypt. They are in the most degraded state, and their wretched condition has effaced every trace of antiquity. Only the hatred of the Tulmudists to the Karaites has been inherited. Of the latter there are said to be two hundred here, one hundred and fifty in Jerusalem, eighty in Tiberias, two hundred in Damascus, and one thousand five hundred in Constantinople, and who for the same reason offer nothing worthy the attention of the enquirer, except the peculiar formation of their scull.

An accurate acquaintance with the Jews in Abyssinia, whose existence is confirmed by many authorities, would be important in other respects than the mere gratification of curiosity. An ambassador sent one hundred and fifty years ago from the Prince of Sana to the Emperor of Abyssinia, also saw them confined to the recesses in the mountains. They lead a wandering life, subsist by breeding cattle, have the Sabbath, circumcision eight days after the birth, and no religious book but the Pentateuch. According to the accounts given by the leaders of caravans, the Jews in the interior of Africa equally incline to Theism, and their Cohens are said to be as unacquainted with the Hebrew, as the Christian priests in the east are with Greek. Tradition tells of three great Jewish caravans that went to Abyssinia under the reign of King Solomon; the first with the natural son of Solomon and the Queen of Sheba; of an active commercial intercourse between the two kingdoms; of the conversion of Abyssinia to the Jewish religion; and of a sanguinary war between the Jews and Christians in the fifth century, in which the former were almost wholly exterminated in Abyssinia, only a few having escaped by flight, into the interior of Africa. Now whether they had previously been led by commerce to settle in the interior, or whether this did not take place till their expulsou from Abyssinia, their origin is the same, and they only become the more interesting in an historical point

of view.   But it is to be feared that the contempt in which they
are there held by the heathens and Mahometans, has reduced them
to as deplorable a condition as in the east in general, or as that of
their brethren in Caucasus, in the mountains of Taurus, and even
in Yemen, with whom we are equally unacquainted, is represented.

A considerable number of men in the east still labour under
the curse of being treated and sold like brute beasts.   Most of
them are exported from Egypt to all parts of the Turkish empire, being annually brought by a great caravan from Sennar
and Darfour, and now that travelling is so secure, in several
small caravans to the number of five or seven thousand every
year.   The princes of those countries make war on the neighbouring tribes, and the result generally is the taking of several thousand
prisoners.   Part of them are employed to cultivate the land and
tend the camels in the country itself; the others are sold or bar-
tered as slaves to the caravans, like ivory, gum, ostrich feathers,
rhinoceros horns, alum, &c.; the number of the prisoners is increased by those sold by their barbarian parents.   On the journey
these poor wretches are most dreadfully ill-treated, and as soon as
they arrive at Cairo exposed to sale in the slave market, where
from eighty to two hundred dollars are paid for them, according
to their ability, age, strength and beauty.   I observed that the
women, who generally make above three-fourths of the number,
endeavour to heighten their attractions, chiefly by braiding their
hair in a very beautiful manner.   They are employed as domestic
servants, but it is difficult to teach them.   Their lot is generally
more tolerable under Turkish masters than under Franks, but
very different from what it is in America.   They are considered
as servants of the house, and frequently when they conduct themselves well and give proofs of ability, as members and friends of
the family.   Among the Franks the possession of them is generally attended with loss, as they have more liberty, the females
soon become pregnant, and the males good for nothing and
thievish.   They are likewise more susceptible of the plague than
other persons, as is confirmed by many observations, and of
seventy thousand persons who have been carried off by the plague,
within a few years, fourteen thousand were slaves.   It is difficult,
and generally impossible, to obtain any information from them
respecting their native country and language, as they have generally been brought away when very young, and have no recol-
lection of it.   As Volney and others have given very good accounts of the Mahometan tribes, I conclude this chapter with a
remark upon the Gypsies. They are here called Tatar or Aghar.
Their customs are the same as those which distinguish them
among us.   They bury their dead privately.   Here too they
employ themselves in fortune-telling, prophecying, rope-dancing,

tumbling, &c. They are supposed to be Theists, and to have come originally from the interior of Asia.

Abyssinia.

Cairo and Jerusalem are frequented by people from various parts of Asia and Africa, from whom I have collected much information. Some particulars are omitted here, because they have been more perfectly related by preceding travellers. With respect to Abyssinia, which was always the favourite object of my plan, I heard many accounts both true and false. There is nothing more to be regretted than the premature death of the companion of the English consul-general, Mr. Salt, in his travels in Abyssinia.* He resided there eight years, and the situation in which he was placed gives us reason to suppose that his knowledge of the country must have been very extensive. There can be no doubt that the journey to Abyssinia from Egypt by land, is extremely fatiguing and difficult, and people always prefer going by sea. I got acquainted with some persons from Axum, who assured me that no Mahometan state had maintained itself there, and that the followers of Mahomet are very few, and even these live and dress like Christians. Shoa, Machedo and Noari are Christian states. The latter is five days journey from the Nile, and the inhabitants speak the Malhas language. There are many other Christian states, and I have a list of above thirty dialects, the people speaking which are all Christians.

The Libraries at Cairo. The Schools and Charitable Institutions. The Legacies to the Mosques. The Prayer of the two Beiram.

The library of Mahomet Ali Pacha, the present governor, will probably soon occupy a distinguished rank among those establishments at Cairo. To the fine collection of Arabic MSS. he exerts himself to add a number of Arabic translations of French and Italian works on mathematics and natural philosophy, and has some chosen Mamelukes educated in the European manner. The library of M. Asselin, a learned Frenchman living in Cairo, contains many rare MSS. But neither the two Latin nor the two Greek convent libraries (those of the Patriarch and of Mount Sinai,) contain any MSS. interesting in a literary view, because they have been always the most exposed to pillage. The most interesting acquisitions in Arabic literature might be made

* Mr. Pearce.

in the libraries of some of the Sheiks. Their treasures, and the
facility with which copies may be procured, will always make
Cairo important to the lovers of Arabic literature. The Darel-
hekmet, now called Dschamea Elazhar, with a considerable
library, which, according to Macrizi, was founded in the year 895,
on the second Dschaumadi, is one of the greatest establishments
for education in the Ottoman empire. It is a very large building, with several piazzas, in which the pupils, to the number of
two thousand, sitting in above one hundred and fifty different
divisions, receive instruction in reading, writing, grammar, the
koran and the law. Not only the library, but even the school is
inaccessible to Christians. I was twice threatened with the
penalty of death for my curiosity by the Shieks, some of whom
are very well informed and solved many of my doubts. They
gave me the following information respecting legacies to the
mosques. If a rich man dies, either with or without heirs, and
has bequeathed any thing to a mosque for repairs, light, carpets,
or other expences, he leaves the money to the care of some respectable person, a Sheik, Iman, or rich merchant, who secures
it by laying it out in the purchase of houses, lands, &c. The
present Pacha has deprived many mosques, that had been en-
riched by such legacies, of the greater part of their property, yet
there are still in Cairo many that are very well endowed. They
assured me that there never was any difference of opinion respecting
the place where the prayer of the two Beirams shall be performed.
It is only at Mecca that it must be performed in the open air on
the Dschebel Araphat, otherwise always in the mosque. There
is a board, consisting of twelve physicians, which is consulted on
difficult cases. In the mad-house I saw fifteen poor wretches in
chains, each confined to a narrow chamber. They appeared to
be so neglected, that they must become mad in such an abode
if they were not so already. The hospital connected with it is in
a similar state. The orientals have no idea of a judicious ma-
nagement and regulation of philanthropical establishments; the
patient is almost entirely left to himself.

So much has already been said of the principal mosques, the
Hall of Saladin, built in a beautiful Saracenic style, on Memphis,
the pyramids and antiquities of Egypt, that I pass over this
subject, and reserve my remarks for another suitable opportunity.

The Country between Cairo and Gaza.

The most convenient mode of travelling from Cairo to Gaza is
by water, going down the Nile from Cairo to Damietta, and
thence to Jaffa. But as the opportunities of going by sea from
Damietta to Jaffa are rare, people generally prefer going by land,
either by way of Belbeys and El Arish, or by way of Suez. We

chose the more interesting route by Belbeys, Arish, and Gaza.
Half a league from Cairo is Matarieh, where the celebrated syca-
more stands, upon the spot in which the Holy Family is said to
have reposed; and in the neighbourhood is the seite of the ancient
Heliopolis, where there is an obelisk and several sarcophagi. We
remarked here the contrast between the most fertile plains in the
world and the desert. On the left are the finest clover and corn
fields, groves of palms, and the most luxuriant vegetation; on the
right nothing but chains of naked limestone hills, which run into
innumerable branches. Halke, four leagues from Cairo, is a
pretty large village, and between that and Belbeys are several
others, in a very picturesque country. The road from Belbeys
to Karein (Coraem?) runs almost constantly between gardens,
and the villages stand very close together. The country is less
populous four leagues beyond Karein, between Chatara and
Salehhieh, where fertile spots and even groves of palms, which,
however, have a connexion with the plain, which is annually
watered by the canals from the Nile, alternate with sterile deserts,
bounded at a distance by a chain of naked mountains. The
country beyond Salehhieh is only occasionally visited by Bedouins. Two leagues farther is the valley of Kantara, with a salt
soil, formed by two chains of hills, that sometimes run parallel,
and in which there are some salt ponds and a well of good water.
After leaving this valley, which is eight leagues in length, the soil
is sandy, and almost entirely barren. Near Catieh there are many
palm trees, and the ruins of a village, which the Arabs affirm to
have belonged to the Jews. El Arish lies in a very fruitful country, and beyond it are the frontiers of Egypt and Syria. For
the space of two leagues you see on all sides an uneven country,
full of herds of cattle grazing, and here and there fine corn fields,
in an extensive plain. After proceeding some leagues further you
perceive the ruins of the town of Rafah, and a very large and
deep cistern of the same name. The country becomes mountainous, and at the foot of the mountains is Chanus, (Khan
Jouness) the ancient Jenysus, the first village in Syria. The
country from Arish to Gaza is low and almost level, to the distance of four leagues from the sea. At a short distance there is a
slope, the country becomes mountainous and more barren, and
you are soon in a desert. We saw no quadrupeds except boars,
hares, and jackalls, which the inhabitants say are very numerous.
The soil is very fertile in this tract, but, especially between Arish
and Gaza, only to the distance of six or eight leagues from the
sea, where the desert begins.

Remains of the Ancient Inhabitants.—The Present Inhabitants.

This whole tract has little that interests the antiquarian. Almost every trace of the ancient inhabitants has been effaced by their barbarous successors. In the middle of the village, at Karein, there is a large isolated block of granite, with ancient Egyptian figures. The present state of the ruins near Bir Catieh does not enable me to judge whether they are ancient; but it is probable that the town of Cheres was near that place.

Of Rhinocorura, now Arish, not a trace remains. A league beyond Arish, and a league from the sea, upon an eminence, there was formerly, it is said, a great Arab village, called Matal, of which nothing remains but the ruins of an aqueduct. At Vadi Rafah, twelve leagues beyond Arish, there are to the left of the road two lofty columns of black granite still standing, and three hundred paces from them a large and deep cistern, which is repaired with pillars of marble and granite. These are the poor remains of that once handsome Christian city, whose former splendour is still recorded in the memory of the Arabs. In the same manner the barbarians have destroyed the remaining antiquities in Khan Jouness, and especially those in Dir Belach, which were very considerable. A league before you reach Gaza are the remains of a bridge, which was built very strong and high, and was probably a work of the Romans. It is over the Dschiser Gaza, which comes from the mountains, and falls into the sea about a league off, but is generally without water.

The present inhabitants of the desert tract from Cantara to Arish are Bedouins, who are tributary to the Pacha of Egypt, and differ but little from those of the Mareotic territory: they are very few in number, and I saw in the whole district only one camp, which was at Vadi Cantara. Arish has three hundred inhabitants, and Khan Jouness above a thousand. Both are fortified as a protection to the frontiers, and the first is celebrated on account of the battle fought near it during the French invasion. They prosper by the trade which they carry on between Egypt and Syria: the inhabitants are remarkably rich in camels; and both demand of the Christians and Jews who pass by, the tribute called Ghafar, which the Mahometan thinks himself authorized to demand of the infidels, especially at certain places.

The fruitful and cultivated tract between Arish and Khan Jouness is inhabited only by Bedouins, who seem, however, to be more prosperous, and to approach to the village life. Many sepulchres are seen in this district, which are as solidly built as those of the inhabitants of the towns. Though the inhabitants of Khan Jouness are much addicted to robbery, those of Dirbelach are said to be very well disposed. They receive both Christians and Mahometans very hospitably, and give them at least some of their dates, of which they gather annually a large quantity, which is exported to Syria. Hence many caravans now proceed along the sea-coast, and this route is now more frequented than that through Khan Jouness.

The religion, both of the Bedouins and the inhabitants of the villages, is the Mahometan. Each village and each camp has at its head a Sheik, who conducts it, directed by the advice of the elders.

From Arish to Gaza the inhabitants are tributary to the Pacha of Acre, or to his Motsallem at Gaza, and those of Egypt, as far as Arish, to Mahomet Ali. Since the campaign to Mecca against the Wechabites, a part of the Bedouins on the east coast of the Red Sea, and in Arabia, are likewise tributary, and the bold hordes of banditti are succeeded by poor weak Bedouins.

Remarks on the Natural Peculiarities of Palestine and a Part of Syria.

The chain of mountains which traverses all Syria extends also in various branches and ramifications to Palestine. They enclose many deep valleys in all directions, and have the most diversified forms, directions and elevations. In Judea most of them are conical; in Samaria flat and elongated; there steep or oblique, lofty or low; here covered with earth, there entirely bare. Great and little Hermon and Tabor are here the highest. Mount Nuris, one league south of Little Hermon, is not so regularly formed as that mountain. In Galilee the valleys are broad and long, branch out in the same manner into manifold ramifications and are very fertile. Petrifactions of plants, olives, and other fruits are found in Kesrouan and on Carmel in a space of half a square league extent, called the Garden of the Mother of God, but the quantity is diminished since they have been so much sought after. Near the grave of Rachel of Bethlehem, great numbers of small stones are found, which in size and appearance exactly resemble peas, and the place is hence called Dscherumel homes, the pea-field. The popular belief attaches great miracles to both these places, by which the holy family, to punish the avaricious inhabitants, transformed all the fruits in their gardens and fields into such stones.

On the dead sea, particularly on the south-west shore, asphaltum is found, which when rubbed emits a sulphureous smell, burns like pitch, and is manufactured by the inhabitants of Jerusalem into crosses, rosaries, &c.

The inhabitants have no idea of mines of metal, though, it is not improbable there may be some in Samaria and Galilee. Iron

is abundant in Antilibanus and Kesrouan. On the sea-shore there
are many greenish stones that look like glass, covered with a rind,
or grown together with limestone, and extremely solid. I saw a
great quantity of them near the ruins of Apollonia; perhaps
they gave occasion to the invention of glass. Palestine is very
rich in saltpetre; I found the sides of the caves of Gethsemane
and other places covered with it.

In the valley of the Jordan, and about the Dead Sea, there are
still traces of volcanos. In the mountains near the Dead Sea we
saw many yellow stones which contain sulphur, ashes also, at a
very considerable distance, and pumice stone in the Dscheser
(river) Ascalon. Half a league to the south of Tiberias and
Hammi there are sulphureous springs. Near Tiberias water
issues from the ground in four places, about five paces from each
other: the water is so hot that one cannot bear to hold a finger in
it more than a few seconds. Those of Hammi, three leagues
more to the south, are not so warm, but they are more visited by
rheumatic patients.

The soil is of very different qualities, but never so rich as with
us; that of the mountains is rough and stony, that of the plains
light and very fertile. In Judæa it is stony and not so warm as
in other parts, and every thing is therefore less forward; but it is
astonishing to see when the weather is favourable, how trees,
shrubs and plants flourish in the seemingly poor soil, and even
in the clefts of the rocks. They never think of improving the
ground by manure, and dung is used by them for fuel.

Palestine, like all mountainous countries, abounds in water.
The Lake of Tiberias, the Jordan, and other rivers, derive their
waters from Lebanon. The other small rivers (Dscheser) are
filled in rainy weather from the mountains, or from springs, the
comparatively small number of which, made cisterns necessary
even in the remotest ages. The most interesting of all the waters
is the Dead Sea, called by the inhabitants Baher Ellut. Even
in the most ancient times it attracted the attention of the observer, and so many fables were related of it, that it was difficult
to distinguish the truth from fiction. It is eleven miles long and
five broad.* Around it are bare mountains, which when sur-
veyed from the eminences present a frightful prospect. Those
on the east are steeper and higher, those on the west more numerous and gloomy. To the north is the plain, four leagues in
breadth, which is traversed by the Jordan. On the banks is an
ash-grey salt, adhesive slime, sand mixed with salt and nitre, or
stones which are covered with a white salt crust. The same is

---

* The author means, we suppose, German mile, equal to four and a half
English.

the case with the great heaps of stones, where lime, flint and
bitumen lie one upon the other and hard by a large spot with
plants growing on it, particularly the Salsola and Salicornia. Many
trunks and branches of trees, which the Jordan has carried into
the sea, and which have been cast up by its waves, are found to be
corroded through and through, and partly converted into a black
mass. Shells, snails, shrubs and other objects have been carried
into the sea by the Jordan. Their distance from the water,
which is as much as thirty paces, shews how violent the south-east
winds are which agitate this sea. Various animals, chiefly locusts
and birds, have perished in the sea, and likewise cover the shores.
The inhabitants have collected heaps of salt on the salt plains
about the sea. The water has such a salt and pungent taste,
that drinking it takes away the breath and occasions sickness at
the stomach. While I strolled along the shore, the south-east
wind blew very strong, and I felt several times as if I were on
the point of suffocation. I thought of the little animals that stray
hither and go blindly to meet their death, flying forward till
they become faint and dizzy and fall in. The few insects creeping on the shore were likewise so faint that it was evident they
had not long to live : but large birds flew boldly round and over
it. On the east shore there are bituminous and sulphureous
springs, which are called by the inhabitants the baths of Moses,
David and Solomon. When we consider all these phenomena, we
cannot but acknowledge that this sea and the environs have many
peculiarities which are simply and satisfactorily illustrated by the
narrative of the sacred historian. In the midst of these bare limestone rocks there was an Oasis, with a salt soil and salt springs like
Siwa, but far superior in fertility and salubrity on account of the
fine water of the Jordan. There was a volcano, the subterraneous
hollows of which undermined the Oasis. Bituminous and sulphureous springs issued from the south-east side of the Oasis,
streams of lava from the western side, till the anger of God fell on
this country ; a tempest set fire to the subterraneous combustible
substances, the surface sunk in, and the fruitful tract was
changed into a lake, which is impregnated with all the above-
mentioned substances, especially salt. The Jordan is about ten
paces broad, flows very rapidly, and has its banks quite covered
with trees. At the place where the pilgrims bathed it forms an
island. There are many rivulets which have no water except in
the winter, when they are at times so deep, that hardly a year
passes without some persons being drowned in them.

Near most of the towns and villages there are springs, which
being in the valleys, while the villages are on the hills, it is a chief
occupation of the women to fetch the water into the village. Near
the sea the water in the springs is often brackish. At Jaffa it

contains much nitre, and they are obliged either to bring better water from a distance by means of aqueducts, as at Acre, Sur, and Saida, or to collect the rain water in cisterns.

St. Mary's well in the valley of Jehosaphat (perhaps formerly called the spring of Siloah) is remarkable for having, at certain times, hardly any water in it, and soon after a large quantity. People bathe in it, because it is said to have a healing virtue, especially for the eyes. Above twenty steps lead down to it, and a subterraneous channel leads it into the pond of Siloah. Several flights of steps, above ten feet deep, lead down into this also. It is twenty feet broad, and twenty-five feet long.

Not far from it is the well of Nehemiah (now called Bir Ajub) which is above one hundred and thirty feet deep. It was probably imagined that by digging so deep they would reach a spring, but this has proved to be a mistake. A greater quantity of water is thus collected, but that does not hinder its being nearly exhausted when the season is very dry, though it sometimes overflows in very rainy winters.

What Volney says of two principal climates in Syria, is less applicable to Palestine, because the mountains are not so high. Yet the vicinity of Lebanon has considerable influence, and if the temperature of the summer is nearly the same on the sea coast and on the mountains, that of the winter is different. It is colder in the mountains, piercing winds and rain are more frequent, and snow sometimes falls. In 1820 it lay in Galilee only four hours. In 1818, at the end of January, it lay for five days, two feet deep; and in 1796 it lay also in Judæa several days, such a depth that it came into the doors of most of the houses. Hail is not uncommon in winter. While I was at Nazareth there were several showers of hail, and the stones were as large as pigeon's eggs. It is said to have been remarked that hail is most frequent in those years when it does not snow. The rainy months are from November to March, both inclusive. It seldom rains in October and April, and never in the other months. The rising of the water in the well of Nehemiah, furnishes in Judæa a standard for general meteorological observations. The water rose so as to overflow, in the years 1814, 1815, 1817, 1818, 1819, (three times) 1821, (twice) and in 1815 and 1821 in great abundance. These were wet but fruitful years. In 1816 and 1820 it could hardly be perceived that the water in the well had risen. The cisterns were exhausted, and famine, drought, and diseases ensued. In heavy rains large masses of clouds are observed, some floating in the air, some enveloping the mountains, which, after the rain, or when the atmosphere is only overcast, appear, from the light motion of the clouds, as if they smoked. In general, no clouds are seen throughout the summer; they do not appear till October, and generally come from the north-west, north, or north-east. In those months the fog is often very thick in the morning and evening, and sometimes the whole day, and the night dews are heavy. The air on the mountains is light, pure, and dry, but in some valleys, for instance near the sea of Tiberias, and on the coast of the Mediterranean, it is damp, and in many places, as for example, near Ascalon, so unwholesome that the inhabitants were obliged to change their abode. In Antura also, and other parts of the Kesrouan, it is necessary in the summer months to retire into the mountains to escape the fever. Similar complaints were made at Beirout previously to the planting of the grove of pines, and are still made at Acre, where the exhalations from the neighbouring marshes may be the cause, and at Jaffa, where fevers prevail in some months of the year.

The winds are nearly as periodical in Palestine as in Egypt. In the winter months the north, north west, and north east winds, the harbingers of rain, predominate. In February and March they blew very violently almost every day, the atmosphere was overcast, the air cold and damp, and for twenty years or more there has not been so much rain as this year. The heat of the summer is generally mitigated by the west wind on the mountains.

There are never any thunder storms in summer, but frequently in the winter months. On the 5th of March, 1821, there were two near Acre, the wind being NE., on the 27th of February a very violent one, and another equally violent on the 15th of March at Naplous. At the end of January there were two at Jerusalem; and two at the beginning of March at Nazareth. They come from Lebanon with a north east wind, and seldom do any damage. The meteors called falling stars are as frequent here as they are in Egypt. Ali Bey says he saw at Jerusalem a meteor which shot from east to west. An old man at Nazareth told me that about forty years ago, a flame of fire was seen, which fell from the heavens on the ground, burst and caused great terror.

Earthquakes are extremely rare in Palestine. About twenty-five years ago, the shock of one was felt at Nazareth, which is said to have been of several seconds duration.

Palestine is very rich in vegetable productions; even the rude rocks of Judæa are full of them, and covered in winter with beautiful verdure. Numerous plants that grow wild are used for food. They almost all blossom from February to April. There is no want of trees. The pomegranate is common : it blossoms in July and the fruit ripens in October. Besides the species with sweet fruit, there is another, the fruit of which is sour, but there is no difference in the blossoms or the leaves. The olive blossoms in April, and the crop is gathered in September. The oil is not so good as it might be, because they are obliged to gather the fruit before it is ripe to preserve it from the thieves. The most considerable palm-grove is near Derbelach; there are likewise several near Gaza, but in Rama, Acre and Jerusalem, they are less frequent. The principal forests are still in Lebanon, Antilebanon, and in the valley near Halil. It is not merely in the variety of their productions, but also in the luxuriance of their vegetation, that Syria and Palestine excel most of the provinces of the Ottoman empire, though no great labour is bestowed in the culture of the soil.

Cotton, tobacco, beans and lentils are sown in March, after the ground has been well broken with a plough or spade. The grains of cotton are first stirred for a time in wet ashes, or in red earth, to promote their rapid growth. They are sown in rows, the weeds carefully pulled up and the earth loosened with a spade. In July the pods are gathered and the haulm left on the field. Where the soil is moist they sow cotton every year, otherwise only every two or three years. As soon as they have peeled off the husk of the cotton, they separate it from the seeds by a machine, in which two cylinders, one made of wood, and large, the other of iron, are set in motion, in contrary directions, by means of a wheel. The wool winds through, the seeds remain behind, and are said to be very good for oxen. I remarked in some places, that corn, even when already in the ear, was used as fodder for horses; it is said to make them strong and fat. The vine blossoms in May and the grapes are ripe in August. They are usually dried, or a kind of decoction made of the must; for only the Christians make wine.

Of wild animals the most common are the *kanzes, gazal, arneb, chanzier and Abuelchisani.* The wool of the sheep is coarse, and is manufactured in the towns; it is mixed with cotton and made into carpets or ordinary clothing. Oxen and cows are used in agriculture. Their hides are said not to be strong enough for use, nor do the people know the usual manner of preparing them. In the day time, the dogs are out of the towns, and often in the church-yards, and bark furiously at those who pass by. But in the night each goes to his own quarter of the city, which he will not suffer to be contested with him by any one. If a strange dog comes into it, the neighbours immediately come to the help of the one whose dominion has been trespassed on, and woe be to the stranger if he does not immediately take flight. The Arabs feed them, but carefully avoid touching them. In general they resemble our shepherd dogs. In Jericho they are large, lean, and like our greyhounds. Almost all kinds of birds that we have in Germany abound in Syria, especially birds of prey. Amphibious animals are less numerous, and the report that Tiberias and Saffet were once uninhabitable on account of the number of snakes is not now confirmed. The inhabitants unanimously affirm that the Jordan, and still more the sea of Tiberias, abound in fish. The breeding of bees is carried on here with as great advantage as it is in Egypt. There they make more wax, here more honey. Very little care is bestowed on them, but they make a great deal of honey, and that of Bethlehem is celebrated for its whiteness and good flavour. The wax is far from sufficient for the consumption, and the pilgrims from Cardistan and Anatolia bring large quantities to Jerusalem. If they do not come, a high price must be paid for that of Egypt. The Arabs have no want of fleas and lice, and Acre and Saffet are said to be particularly well stocked with them. Caterpillars are innumerable. In February, March and April, they are seen on the ground in rainy weather, in clumps, under a web. Near Gaza the ticklouse is very common. It flies into people's faces, eats itself in, and immediately becomes giddy and dies. If it fastens on the foot or any other part of the body, it often lives two days, but still dies after boils have broken out on the body.

The locusts are a well known plague of Syria and Palestine. They generally come, after a warm winter, from the deserts of Arabia. Two years ago they consumed at Heifa, and last year at Nazareth, not only all the grass, but even the shoots of the trees and the pease and other leguminous vegetables in the bazar. Three years ago they thrice visited Jerusalem in great numbers. This year they arrived so early as the 6th of April, two days after a strong south wind. A single one lays one hundred eggs. To attempt their destruction by burning or burying is considered to be of no use. They are therefore left to take their course till they either fly to another place of their own accord, or are whirled away by the east wind, which is their most dangerous enemy. They are strung upon a thread and dried for food.

The great fertility of Palestine causes all kinds of provisions to be very cheap. In Samaria the prices are usually rather higher, and in Judæa the highest of all. Here too people complain of high prices and bad times. Several old persons gave me a comparative statement of the prices, which shewed that they had encreased six-fold within fifty years. At Jerusalem this is ascribed to the increased number of the pilgrims. Formerly there came at Easter hardly five hundred, and now above four thousand.

Fertile as this country always was and still is, yet it resembles (in one part) a solitary desert. Whence, the reader may ask, is this phenomenon? About fort years ago the Pacha of Damascus, disguised as a dervise, and accompanied by one of his confidants, travelled through the country about Jericho. They were hospitably treated. The inhabitants set all kinds of provisions before them, and gave them juice of the sugar-cane in a dish. A single stem was sufficient to fill a whole dish with juice. The Pacha inferred from the fertility of the country that the inhabitants must be rich, and loaded them with heavy taxes. He sent soldiers there every year to levy the tribute which he asked, who ill-treated the people and extorted thrice as much as was required.

The inhabitants, weary of this oppression and ill-usage, almost all fled with their property into the desert. After a lapse of many years, the Pacha again visited the country, and was astonished at finding it so desolate and barren. Instead of a single sugar-cane, ten were required to fill half a dish. He relieved the country from tribute, but the fugitives did not return, and thus one of the most beautiful parts of Palestine has become almost a desert. This is the history of all the provinces of the Turkish empire, and those which are not yet converted into a waste, may expect that this will be their fate.

Ruins in Palestine and on the Coast of Phœnicia.

There are few countries so abounding in traces of a former great population, but few also where they are so uninteresting as in Palestine. The finest buildings are destroyed to the very foundations, and it is only of ordinary houses, that some insulated walls remain standing. Most of them are of the times of the Romans, and so insignificant that they would not deserve notice, were not their names, though very much disfigured, of importance to ancient geography and history. The villages of Kawata, Zaka, Lebhem, marked on Danville's map, have long since wholly disappeared.

At Gaza there are but few remains. In the town and before it, are ancient vaults: in the burying ground of the Mahometans there are marble slabs with very ancient inscriptions. In Azot there are still many old walls: in Jebna the ruins of a church, afterwards converted into a mosque, but now forsaken and partly destroyed. In the valley westward there is an aqueduct, cisterns and bridges.

On the whole sea-coast the ruins of Ascalon and Cæsarea are the most considerable. Those of Ascalon, in their present state, do not carry us back to the times of the Romans. Two years ago Lady Stanhope employed workmen to dig, but the only fruit of her great expences, was some statues of the times of the Romans, and these she had broken, to remove a prejudice of the inhabitants, who thought that treasures were hidden in them. It is probable that a more satisfactory result might be obtained by digging in old Cæsarea. Here there are gigantic columns of granite and marble, prodigious walls half buried, which inspire melancholy reflections on the vicissitudes of things. In this elevated spot, which is four hundred paces long and as many broad, the *Turris Stratonis* probably stood, which Herod, according to Josephus, adorned with a magnificent palace.

The extraordinary splendour of Cæsarea may be further inferred from the more considerable remains of New Cæsarea. Besides the lofty strong city walls and many buildings, there are columns by hundreds on the sea-shore one above another, or lying close together in the water. In every one of these remains, we see the magnificence of Old Cæsarea, the ruins of which furnished the materials. Great quantities of marble blocks and columns have since been carried to Acre and Jaffa to build the fortifications. There are also many remains of walls and of single houses, without the abovementioned walls, on the sea-coast to the north. The ruins of a convent at Der Asnid, a league north of Gaza, which lie scattered over a large field, deserve notice. Two leagues south of Jaffa are the ruins of the lofty bridge with two arches, under which the little river Rubin flows. The prodigious size of the stones, and the height of the arches, render it very remarkable and shew it to be of great antiquity. There are two chapels near it in which the Mahometans perform their prayers. Near Jaffa, on the way to Rama, are the considerable ruins of an ancient mosque called Hedra.

Three hundred paces to the west of the present town of Rama, are the ruins of a large building now called Dschamea Elabidh, and formerly the Church of the Forty Martyrs. This building, which is six hundred paces in length and breadth, was erected by the Knights Templars in the times of the crusades. We even still see the upper and the subterraneous church with nine pillars and two naves, the subterraneous dwellings, magazines and cisterns, the external walls and the cells.

In later times the Arabs made three mosques in it, as appears from the inscriptions, one on the north and two on the south side of the square edifice, and built in the middle two chapels for Santons. The upper wall of the lofty minaret, the ascent to which is by a hundred and twenty-five steps, is far inferior in solidity and beauty to the lower part built by the Christians. Some years ago, the Mostalem wished to use these large and handsome stones for building, but he could not get one of them entire, and therefore desisted from his purpose. It is now two hundred years since it was ruined. The cistern of St. Helena, probably built by her, is very deep and uncommonly large, being thirty-three feet in length and thirty in breadth, with twenty-four openings, and constructed with great solidity.

In the Dschamea Kebir, now the largest mosque in the town, the great church of St. John is easily recognized, only the mina-

ret is of Saracen architecture. The subterraneous vaults are also
remarkable which are near the convent of the Franks, and always
contain much water in the wet season. They were discovered
fifteen years ago, but the people were so terrified at their depth
and extent, that they immediately bricked them up again. They
are said to be like a labyrinth, and were probably reservoirs for
water, but the present inhabitants had no notion of the use for
which they were intended.

Near Haram are the considerable remains of Apollonica. You
see, in the sea, large thick walls, and close to them, handsome
stairs, which lead from the lower buildings to the upper ones,
situated on 'the high bank. Of these there are still considerable
remains, the solidity and construction of which seem to indicate
that a castle once stood here. Granite and marble columns are
in the sea, and fragments of walls scattered in the adjacent fields.
It is probable, that by digging, the ancient walls of the city
might be traced. Five hundred paces north of Tantura, on the
sea, are the ruins of a considerable castle, which the inhabitants
say was built by the French during the crusades.

This whole country, as far as Atlid, was formerly full of
castles, houses, and cisterns, but most of the first are totally destroyed, and the latter filled up: only a castle, on the ridge of
the adjacent chain of mountains, still remains. On Mount Carmel are numerous caves, which may have formerly served as
dwellings for hermits. The largest of them, called the School of
Elijah, is held in great veneration by the Mahometans and Jews.
The cave, which is eighteen paces long, and ten broad, is guarded
by an Iman. All round there is a bench for the Divan, except
on the left side, in the middle of which there is a similar grotto,
five paces long, and as many broad, less regularly hewn in the
rock. At the back part of the larger division there are lamps,
and some rags, which are called trophies of victory, and are most
devoutly touched by the Mahometans who come hither on pilgrimage. Several came in while I was there: they prayed first
at the door, then in the middle, lastly near the lamps, and concluded their devotion by kissing the flags. The Mahometans
and Jews call this the School of Elijah; that above, in the convent, the School of Elisha. The Greek inscriptions carved in the
two side walls are very old, and merit the attention of those who
study Greek paleography. The contents of all are the same. Each
of those who have carved their names beg to be remembered.
They were probably made in the first centuries, of the Christian
era, by persons who visited these holy places out of devotion.

The ruins of the celebrated Carmelite convent are on Mount
Carmel. It was rebuilt ninety years ago. The buildings were
formerly more extensive. The ruins which are now seen, among

which are blocks of marble, are said to be as old as the times of
St. Helena: that they are older than the Crusades seems certain. During the French invasion the convent was used as an
hospital: all the soldiers wounded at the siege of Acre were conveyed thither, and many perished in the retreat. The convent
was plundered, and the church stripped of its roof by the troops
of Ghezzar Pacha. A hundred steps to the north-west is a
chapel, built about sixty years ago, by the schismatic Greeks.
Almost in the middle of the plain of Acre, on a mountain, there
is a very ancient building, near which are many substructions.
An ancient paved road, probably a work of the Romans, leads
nearly to it. About Acre you find several columns of marble
and granite; but in the immediate vicinity of the city, every monument of antiquity has been cleared away in erecting the fortifications. In the city itself there are still many monuments, chiefly
of the time of the crusades. The Phœnicians called it Acca, also
Abyron or Accaron; the Greeks called it Ptolemaîs, and the
Romans, Civitas Acconensis. The Knights of St. John, in the
Crusades, gave it the name of St. Jean d'Acre. On the *Raas el
Mescherfi* (Scala Tyriorum), there are various substructions and
reservoirs for water, which seem to be of high antiquity. They
are not of the times of the crusades. This was probaby the
frontier of the Phœnician territory, and an important point.
The Castellum Lamberti is at the foot of Mount Saron, near the
village of the same name. A league distant, six hundred
paces from the sea, on an eminence, is a great number of columns
with doric capitals, some standing, others lying on the ground.
These are, undoubtedly, remains of the very ancient town of
Sida. A league further are the much more remarkable ruins of
Ecdippa. Large and small marble columns, solid foundations,
&c., show that this was a much richer and more important place.
From this place we see a broad road made with stones almost to
Cape Blanco. As soon as you have got round Cape Blanco,
where the road is continually steep and dangerous, you again
find remains of a very considerable place, with cisterns.

The under wall of the Well *Raaselain,* called also Solomon's
Well, is certainly of the remotest ages; and in the neighbouring
village of the same name, there are many walls of great solidity
and high antiquity. An aqueduct, which is partly destroyed,
leads from hence to the ancient Sur. That part is best preserved
which leads from the Mosque Maschuk nearly to the present
town of Sur. The hand of man has not yet been able to efface
here every trace of more enlightened times. The most considerable ruin in the city, is that of a great church of the Byzantine
age. We still distinguish the arches, the bold construction, the
height; and near it are some granite columns of prodigious size.

On the way from Sur to Saida, we meet with considerable remains of some town, almost every half league, and the nearer we approach the latter place, the more evident traces do we find of its ancient splendour. Three leagues before Saida, are the ruins of Sarepta, near which is the oratory of Elijah. Five years ago, a sarcophagus was found two leagues from Saida, but the inscription has been since wantonly destroyed. About Saida there are many remains of walls and columns, but nothing of importance; and the ruins in the city itself are uninteresting, and of the rudest ages.

In general, we cannot take a step here without being reminded of ancient and more prosperous times. Sometimes you meet with cisterns half filled up; sometimes with fragments of marble columns; and the cattle graze, or the corn now grows, where cities, villages, and gardens once presented the most gratifying scenes of animation, industry and opulence.

Ruins in Galilee.

The ruins of Diocæsarea are very considerable. Many columns of granite, fragments of walls and marble lie scattered about the mountain, and at its foot where Saphuri now stands. In Nazareth; near the church of the Latin convent, there are ancient columns, capitals, &c. of a larger size, and in most of the remaining houses, substructions of a better age. On Mount Tabor are many ruins chiefly of the times of the crusades. In and about Tiberias, we found ruins and columns which attest the splendour that it received from Herodes Antipas. These remains are particularly important on the east side to the distance of half a league beyond Tiberias. The city, in ancient times, was more to the south, and it is only since the crusades that it has stood on its present seite. Remains of temples and other great buildings may still be traced, but I looked in vain for inscriptions.

Among the antiquities in the city I observed an alto relievo on a stone of blue granite, which may have been placed over the door of a house. It is four feet long, one and a half high and upwards, the same subject twice over; a lion biting a lamb in the hind leg. The similarity with the Phœnician style made this monument interesting to me, though the rudeness of the workmanship is by no means pleasing.

Where the Jordan issues from the sea of Galilee, there are considerable remains of walls on both banks, which appear to me to be of the times of the crusades. Not far off there are remains of a bridge of the times of the Romans, which are in such a state, that no great expense would be necessary to repair the bridge, by which many travellers would be saved the trouble of wading through the Jordan, which after heavy rains is attended with danger, as ocular demonstration has proved to me. In Hamur are the ruins of Codolara, among which those of the Roman amphitheatre are the most remarkable for their extent and good state of preservation.

Ruins in Samaria.

In Dschenin, there are many ruins which appear to be chiefly of the times of the Saracens: the most important is a khan, built five or six hundred years ago, and destroyed about fifty years ago. It consisted of four parts, the court yard, the dwellings, the seraglio and the mosque. Part of the walls are still standing, with the great gateway, over which sentences from the koran are carved in alto-relievo in Neski characters, recommending to the rich to take care of the poor.

Immediately beyond Dschenin, in the narrow valley, the remains of a tower are seen on a mountain to the right. Such remains are common in Samaria, but there are none in such good preservation as these. The lower walls of most of the houses in Samaria are very ancient. On the way from Naplous to Samaria (Sebaste) there are remains of an aqueduct, and in Sebaste itself many marble columns, most of them lying on the ground, many standing, but without any inscriptions. The ruins of the church of St. John the Baptist, which the Mahometans have partly converted into a mosque, are the most considerable. To the west are the ruins of Marta Azor. At Naplous there are in the houses many pillars of granite and marble, and walls which are the work of more prosperous times: near it is Jacob's well and many ruins. In Sendschel there are many ruins of the most ancient times, and a great many old towers. At Elbir, the ancient Machmas, there are many old walls, among which we distinguish those of a large church built by St Helena, on the spot where the parents of Christ discovered that their son had remained behind at Jerusalem. At Kariataneb (St. Jeremia), are the ruins of a church, which has not been used as such for these two hundred years: it is large, on the whole in good preservation, has much resemblance with a basilica, and is now used as a stable for horses. The grave of Rachael is on the way to Bethlehem, half a league from the convent of Elias, in the plain of Ewata Atantur. Near the grave of Rachael there is a stone on the ground, with the following letters:)ELAVREL.— In Bethlehem there are numerous remains of ancient edifices, but very few that are interesting. The principal church itself is a very remarkable monument of christian antiquity, and the following likewise merit attention; viz. the tomb of St. Jerome, that of St. Paula, and her daughter Eustochia, that of St. Eusebius, abbot of Cremona, near the church of St Catherine, and the sacellum of that great father of the church. The most remarkable ruins near this village, are those of the Om Solomon, the extent and solidity of which claim for this work the antiquity that is ascribed to it. Tradition reports them to have been erected by Solomon, and to be the same with those of Edom. They lie in a valley close to a hill. To the NW. opposite the ponds, is the walled well under ground with a hole, and two other artificial ones. Over it there are great vaults. The aqueduct lies deep in the ground, on a stone foundation. The water flows through round iron pipes, which are covered with two hewn stones, and walled in with stones. There are three ponds. At the foot of the El-feridi mountain of the French, who had a great fortress here, of which many ruins are still visible, are remains of Engaddi; and to the west is the labyrinth of Chareitum. The exterior is of good workmanship, but the interior is but little known. The subterraneous passages are said to extend very far, and to be filled with many wild beasts. Vadi Musa, two days and a half journey NE. of Akaba, is extremely remarkable for the numerous antiquities, and the remains of the ancient city of Petra, which has been frequently visited of late years.

Ruins in and about Jerusalem.

Jerusalem has had the melancholy lot to be so often levelled to the foundations, that the appearance of many parts is quite changed : the extent of mount Sion, and the Moriah, are now difficult to trace ; and it would probably be impossible for the most careful inquirer to discover or accurately to distinguish, among the mass of ruins, the traces of those which belong to particular periods.

Thus we know, that when the Jews began to rebuild the temple after it destruction, the Emperor Adrian caused all the remains to be thrown into the valley, and a grove, consecrated to Jupiter, to be planted there. What was then done to the valley about the Moriah, was done to other valleys, with other buildings; and the valley of Jehosaphat has also lost, by this means, much of its depth, breadth and fertility. The inquirer, therefore, is like one led by an ignus fatuus, goes from one piece of wall to another, in hopes of finding interesting remains, and is every where disappointed. We have, however, certain fixed points in which we cannot be deceived,—the valley of Jehosaphat and Gehenna, the wall of Siloah, the brook of Kedron, mount Sion, the situation of the whole tract, in which we can easily distinguish the ανωτερα and κατωτερα πολις, and even in the ruins of the καινοπολις. The absurdities which would result from any alteration, are evident to

every unprejudiced person. The inhabitants are probably right in
their conjectures also; that the ruins under the present harem,
columns of uncommon size, walls of remarkably large stones,
some walls in the *Birket Israel,* the foundation of the south-east
wall of the city, and some cisterns on mount Sion, are of the age
of David or Solomon; that some pieces of walls about the city,
many filled up vaults in it, a considerable part of the south-east
wall, which surrounds the former temple of Solomon, as well as
the Mosaic pavements, and many ruins under the harem, are of
the times of the Romans. So much appears from the description
given by several Christians, who were employed as workmen in
the reparation of the harem undertaken three years ago, which
had been burnt six years ago, and who of course had to search
every part, that remains dating from various periods may be here
distinguished. If the long passages and large halls, which they
observed in them, were of the age of Herod, the above-mentioned
remains were certainly not so. Reasons, derived from history,
architecture or paleography, lead us to attribute to the times of
the Romans, the tombs of the kings, as they are called, half a
league north-west of the city; also most of the sepulchres hewn
in the rock in the valley of Jehosaphat, and the tombs of the
judges a league to the north-west of Jerusalem.

The only remains of the time of Constantine are the lower part
of the church of the Holy Sepulchre, and a gate on the east side
with many ornaments, the church of the Tomb of the Virgin, and
the wooden door taken from the first, at St. Stephen's gate, or
Setti Mariam. The border, frieze, and all the ornaments are in
the same style, and like others of these times, their age is, therefore, evidently proved, and the tradition confirmed.

Many Greek churches are of the age of Justinian and Heraclius, but either because they had been devastated, or from
other causes, they have undergone considerable alterations.

The ruins of the hospital of the knights of St. John, between
the bazar and the church of the Holy Sepulchre, are of the time
of the crusades. It seems to have resembled a fortress, and was
thrice as large as the Armenian convent, five hundred paces long
and nearly as many broad. When Saladin, favoured by treachery
and good fortune, had already scaled the walls of Jerusalem, the
Christians long defended themselves obstinately in it. At length,
being without succour or hope, they were obliged to yield, and
were all put to the sword. It was hereupon determined, that in
future there should be no building within the walls of this hospital,
and hence this spot, which lies almost in the middle of the city, has
lain waste up to this day. There are merely some small houses with
shops on the east and south sides, where the bazar is. Formerly
they all belonged to the patriarchs of Jerusalem. Some centuries

ago, one of the patriarchs fell so desperately in love with a Turkish girl, that he promised to abjure his religion and embrace Mahometanism if he could obtain the girl for his wife. The Turks, rejoiced at the acquisition of a man of his importance, gave him the girl. The houses remained to him and his descendants, above forty different families of whom now live in Jerusalem. They share among them the revenue of these houses, which, from the increased number of pilgrims, has been augmented within these thirty years in the proportion of 7 to 17. The foundations of this building are, however, much older, and part of them must be referred at least to the time of the Romans. It is possible that even in the time of Constantine the ruins of ancient buildings were made use of in building a palace for the patriarch, remains of which are here to be seen. The patriarchal church was west of the church of the Holy Sepulchre. Part of it is now converted into a mosque. It extended far to the north. The pillars, columns, and arches (behind the church of the Holy Sepulchre) of the ancient church of the apostles, are to be referred to the time of Justinian. On the north-east they joined the building belonging to the clergy of the church of the Holy Sepulchre, and of these also some traces may yet be seen.

The preceding conjectures on the high antiquity of some ruins are by no means arbitrary. The proofs are as strong as can be expected in such a case, and rest on the grand and colossal character which distinguishes all works of remote antiquity. All the accounts and descriptions given by the ancients of the Tower of Babel, the seven wonders of the world, and other equally large buildings, the origin of which the ancients partly involved in ingenious fables, lead us to this conclusion. We have traces of but a very few monuments of these ages remaining for our inspection, and those few are diminutive, compared with the great works which were once erected in all parts of Asia and the north-east of Africa, and even in the east of Europe. But these few fully confirm the testimony of the ancients. In Italy there are remains of another kind, which give strength to our conjectures. They are the Cyclopean walls. These are generally ascribed to the flourishing times of the Etruscan tribes, or even to those ages of which we have no accounts whatever, and nobody will ever think of referring them to the times of the Roman republic, and still less the Augustan age. We consider it equally incorrect to attribute some substructions, which are sometimes met with on Mount Sion, to the Herodian age. From that time downwards, as well as upwards, to the time of Solomon, we find no epoch to which the erection of such gigantic buildings can be well ascribed. The age of the Jebusites or David, and chiefly that of Solomon, are the most suitable. The same criterion guides us when we ascribe the ponds of Solomon, near Bethlehem, to the time of Solomon; the ruins of the bridge of Rubin, some walls of Cæsarea, Sebaste, Sichem, and in all Samaria, the labyrinth near Hebron, and, lastly, some remains under the harem, to times anterior to the Romans, when an energetic national spirit erected them. The well of Nehemiah in the valley of Jehosaphat is also highly interesting to the antiquary ; it is extremely deep, very regularly hewn in the rock, and surrounded above with very solid walls.

The aqueduct is equally interesting, which begins on the south side of this valley, near St. Mary's Well, and proceeds in a straight line to the north-east : it is eight hundred feet long, three and a half high, and two and a half broad. It is built with a solidity that defies destruction. It was destined to convey the superfluous water from the well, and the valley of Jehosaphat, under ground, to the place where the Kedron flows, whence it filled the pond of Siloah, and lies very deep. Above twenty steps lead down to St. Mary's Well. The wall round this well is very old, of very large stones, and some writing of remote antiquity ; but they contain nothing entire, and are almost all defaced.

It would probably be more difficult to fix the age of the remaining ruins, which have been for the most part placed in the state in which we now see them, in the troublesome times of the Abassides, the Fatimites, the Seleucidæ, the crusaders, the Sultans of Egypt, and the Turks. We mention some that are historically remarkable; but must repeat our observation, that the age of most of them has been rendered undistinguishable, either by manifold alterations or too great devastations.

Near the gate Setti Mariam is the Salahijeh, once a church of St. Anne, with a convent of nuns, where St. Anne and the Holy Virgin are said to have been born. It belongs to the Latins, and well deserves to be repaired The Maronites have applied, but in vain, for this fine building. Near the bath Elain was the Church of the Virgin, now there is a press in it, with the mosque Kormi and the tomb of the sheik of that name. Where the principal tan-yard, the most offensive place in Jerusalem, now lies, stood the convent of St. Peter, with a large well-built church, on the spot where the apostles' prison once stood. Not far from the Damascus gate is a large cave, hewn in the rock, which is much venerated by the Christians, Jews, and Mahometans, and on which there was once a convent. Jeremiah is said to have composed his lamentations here. To the south, near the wall, is a small pool, or rather a longish vaulted cistern, which is called the prison of Jeremiah.

Without the present walls of the city, a quarter of a league to the west, is a bath, called Berket Mameleh. It is one hundred and fifteen paces long, seventy-seven broad, in the direction of north and south, and eight feet deep. On the east and west sides there are steps to descend into it. It is difficult to decide at what period the cisterns near it were erected. They are well built, but now filled with human bones. The many ruins in the environs are of different ages, without any peculiar characteristics. The sepulchres hewn in the rock are certainly all of them very old, some filled up, and most of them much damaged. With the hope of finding inscriptions, I crept into most of them, but without success. Almost all of them have a vestibule, a room with a seat or divan, and side apartments, with recesses for the corpses. I found the vestibules in many of them to be six paces broad and four paces long, the entrance three feet high, the room five paces long and as many broad, the divan a foot and a half high. In this part of the country, to the west and north-west, half a league from Jerusalem, I counted about fifty, partly in a line one after the other, partly scattered about. The most celebrated among them, and the nearest to the city, are the tombs of the kings.

The access to them was formerly by a large portal and a flight of steps; now all is destroyed, and the entrance very difficult. You come first into a hall, eight paces square, in which there is a door, leading to the side vaults. There are many pieces of the lids ornamented with flowers in alto-relievo, but only one that is entire. It is five feet and a half long, and the workmanship is good. They are generally ascribed to the Herodian age. Those of the judges, north-west of the latter, are all remarkable for the great number of recesses for bodies, by and over each other. Near them is a great number of tombs, which extend towards the Valley of Lefta. The sepulchres, which are divided from the city by the valley that surrounds Jerusalem, are larger, but partly of later date. Inscriptions in Hebrew and Greek are to be seen on some of them, but for the most part greatly injured. Here were the Phœnician inscriptions already communicated by Clarke and Gau, which I shall explain on another occasion. Many have three crosses, and others a great number carved over the entrance. The number of these sepulchres is very great, and some have large vestibules, which were adorned with paintings, the remains of which shew with certainty that they belong to the period from the fourth to the seventh century, and were destined for Christians. I think that these vestibules were designed for religious meetings, either of single families or of the whole congregation. In the latter case, it must be supposed, that the bones of martyrs or saints repose here. The paintings decide nothing. Christ, the Holy Virgin, and other sacred personages, are represented here in the Byzantine style, as in other Christian paintings of that period, and the principal parts are not yet quite effaced. As these tombs are always so damp, it is surprising that the colours have been preserved so long. There are likewise many such sepulchres about the village of Siloah, to some of which you ascend by ladders. They are of various forms, mostly of good workmanship, and older than those we have just mentioned.

Proceeding from Siloah to the north-west, we came to the present burying ground of the Jews, on the side of the mountain. Here, too, I frequently sought carefully, but could not find any remarkable inscription. There seems to have been but few sepulchres hewn in the rock, on this spot. The most considerable is that of Jehosaphat, which has various apartments. The entablature is in a good taste. It is almost in the middle of the burying ground. More to the south is the tomb of Absalom, with a number of Hebrew inscriptions of latter times, and to the west the tomb of Zachariah, both of a mixed style, and more modern date.

On Mount Sion also there are many sepulchres hewn in the rock, and I was in a fair way of finding some of very great extent. I am of opinion, that by a more accurate investigation, which is impossible under the present government, many subterraneous excavations will be found, older than all the remains which are at present known. This will be proved, not by inscriptions, for these are for the most part destroyed, but by the simple grandeur of the work. The cisterns lately discovered on the top of this mountain, near David's tomb, are large, and admirably contrived; but they will sink into nothing in comparison with the catacomb-like apartments, with which the bowels of Sion are undermined. But those luxuriant corn-fields which clothe Sion in April with the finest verdure, do not conceal only the abodes which have been made out of profound veneration for the dead, but the foundations of buildings, and parts of the walls of the fortress itself. The Christian tombs on it, of all religious parties, and the inscriptions, in the Greek, Latin, and Armenian languages, are uninteresting to the antiquarian, and without importance to paleography. This burying ground, southwards from the Cœnaculum, was always a subject of the most violent disputes between the Christian sects, and all assured me, that it cost them more Spanish dollars than there was room to count upon it. It is believed that St. Stephen, Gamaliel, Nicodemus, and many martyrs of the first centuries are buried here, but no traces of this fact can be found. The Jews, too, have now a burying ground on the south part of Mount Sion, but among the inscriptions, there are none that are ancient.

Ecclesiastical Antiquities in Palestine.

When a critical examination of witnesses respecting the ecclesiastical antiquities of Palestine is talked of, we are led into the domain of the miraculous. But the truth of the tradition, which in memory of interesting scenes in sacred history, made use of such means to prove the circumstances themselves, or the precise spot where they occurred, will, for that very reason, seem suspicious, nay, guilty of forging historical facts, when they are not confirmed by other credible testimony. Hence many learned men have thought fit to consider the theatre of the sacred history, as it is now represented to us, as entirely incorrect, and made alterations, without reflecting that they thereby fell into greater, nay, inextricable difficulties and absurdities. The unprejudiced inquirer will appreciate the proofs deduced from miracles, and the historical facts involved in their Nimbus, because he knows that extraordinary natural phenomena, which, by the special direction of Providence, happened under certain circumstances, that even ordinary events, because they serve as proofs of divine things, are for that reason placed in the class of miracles.

In an age when piety believed that the Christian religion needed them to confirm its divine origin, this happened so often, that esteemed historians of those times certify that most of the important favourable events interwoven with Christianity were connected with miracles. We should therefore have reason to be surprised if the finding of the Holy Cross on which the Saviour of the world completed the great work of the redemption of mankind, and that of places sacred to the Christians, had not been connected with miracles. It was not considered that the most numerous, and by far the most important monuments, were erected by Constantine, or his pious mother Helena, in an age when the truth might still be ascertained from oral testimony. From the age of the apostles men had always lived here, to whom, as friends or enemies of the Christians, these places were not indifferent, who always impressed them on the memory of their descendants, as places sacred to the apostles. Their authenticity is farther attested by a series of respectable Christian writers, who lived in Palestine, and of whom, unfortunately, hardly an thing has been preserved but their names. As they were fond of research, this was a subject that could not be indifferent to them, and they would certainly have corrected by their authority the inaccurate reports of tradition. In the East, too, the common people feel far more interest in antiquity and its traditions, and hence they are preserved with more purity there than in any other country. To cast suspicion on them would be throwing doubts on the whole history of the East, which rests upon them as upon pillars. Lastly, the impartial observer must confess, that the ground, though much changed as we now see it, yet so well agrees with the descriptions of the sacred writers and of Josephus, that we should select the places fixed by tradition, rather than any others, if we had to determine their situation. We will not, therefore, by useless conjectures and reveries, embitter the belief of the millions of pilgrims, but rather thank tradition for having so animated and extended the sphere of their meditations. It is beyond the purpose of this work to justify myself at length on this subject. Other men have done this in folios, and among the many proofs they adduce, there are always some that are irrefragable. I only lament that some places sacred to the Christians have been converted into mosques, and are partly inaccessible to Christians on pain of death ; such are the Temple of Solomon, or that of the Presentation, Mount Sion, where our Saviour celebrated the Holy Sacrament of the Lord's Supper, where the apostles received the Holy Ghost, where Matthew was chosen an apostle, and the first Christian assemblies were held; the arch of Pilate, whence he shewed Christ to the people; and even in part, the place on the Mount of Olives, whence Christ ascended to Heaven; that others lie in ruins, as the Church of the prison of St. Peter, in Jerusalem; the grave of Lazarus in Bethany ; the grotto of the Virgin, and the church of the Shepherds in Bethlehem; the church of St. Joachim and of St. Anne in Saphuri; and the great church of St. Peter in Tiberias, where the scene occurred which is recorded in John xxi.

The church at Cana, in memory of the first miracle; that in memory of the raising of the daughter of Nain; that of the Transfiguration on Mount Tabor, and others: lastly, the church of St. John the Baptist on the Jordan ; all these holy places, together with those that are yet preserved, formed a series, which calls to our memory all the principal acts of our Saviour. At Ain Keram, (St. John) two leagues west of Jerusalem, there is a handsome church, with a chapel on the spot where John the Baptist was born, and with a stone on which he preached. A quarter of a league from it is a well, (Bir Eladri) rendered sacred by frequent visits from St. Elisabeth : a quarter of a league from this, are the ruins of a convent, built by St. Helena, called Dir Elkalbaze, where St. John did penance.

The series of the history of our Saviour begins with Nazareth, the abode of the holy family. The church of the Latins consists of three parts,—the church, the choir, and the sanctuary. The latter is under the choir, and seventeen steps lower than the church, on the seite of the dwelling of St. Joseph. On the left are three pillars, which formed the entrance. The archangel is said to have appeared to the Virgin between the two that stand near together. Behind the third, (the base of which the Turks have broken to pieces, in hopes of finding treasures under it, and which, therefore, hangs suspended to the upper vault) she hid herself, through fear, on hearing the voice of the angel. Behind the altar of this chapel, there are twelve steps, leading to another called the Cave of Safety, to which the holy family retired after their return from Egypt. To the right of the church, and in another excavation on the left, Christ usually performed his prayers. You see there a stone which is always moist. A hundred paces to the north-west of the convent, they shew the work-shop of St. Joseph; three hundred paces south of it, the house in which Christ, with the twelve Apostles, dined; and two hundred paces from that, the Synagogue (now the church of the Catholic Greeks) in which he taught and replied to the Jews, who wished to see the miracles of Capernaum repeated, that they were not worthy of; they were so incensed at this, that they pursued him to the *Mons Precipitii*, half a league east of Nazareth, intending to cast him down, but the rock gave way, and he was able to hold fast in the breaks in the rock, which are still to be seen. When we visit the holy places, we must, in general, be content with the sight of an old wall, or of a hole. Here we are rewarded with a fine prospect into the valley of Esdrelon to Mount Tabor, Hermon, &c. Near the sides of this cleft in the rock, there are cisterns, and ancient walls, and many caves. The first, point out a convent, which the inhabitants say stood there; the last, the dwellings of the Cœnobites. The Holy Virgin had followed her beloved Son at a distance, and when she saw the Jews coming back, she concealed herself, about the middle of the way, in an opening, called, from the fear which she felt, the Cave of Terror. Formerly, there was a convent of nuns here, whence it has, likewise, received the name of Dirbenat.

A league from it is the village of Jaffa, lying on two eminences, in which there is a chapel on the spot where the house of St. James formerly stood. The well, at the foot of the mountain, has its name from it; and near it are considerable remains of a reservoir for fish. I have noticed similar remains near a great many springs in Palestine. On Mount Tabor, besides the remains of a large town, there were, formerly, those of a church, in memory of the Transfiguration of our Saviour. At Cana was the church of St. Bartholomew, and another belonging to the Latins. Formerly, they used to shew the pots that contained the water which Christ transformed into wine.

The field of the ears of corn, (Matth. xii.) almost opposite to the village of Teraam, the Mount of Beatitudes, (Matth. v.)

and the spot where the five thousand people were fed, (Matth. xv. 32, and Mark, viii. 32), have no monument, but tradition has precisely fixed the scene of these transactions : the first place has always been marked by olive trees; the second, is such as could not have been better chosen to awaken pure and elevated sentiments. To the south, is the long and beautiful valley, bounded by the great chain of mountains that extends along the left bank of the Jordan ; to the north, Saffet, with its fertile plain; to the east, the Sea of Tiberias, with its beautiful banks, and to the west, Tabor, and the other mountains of Galilee.

Under the large and handsome church in Bethlehem, of which no use is made, there is a beautiful chapel, richly adorned with good paintings and decorations, on the spot where Christ was born, and where he was worshipped by the Magi. Eastward of the convent, almost at the end of the village, is the grotto of the Holy Virgin; and half a league from it, the field of the Shepherds, *Dschurun Ebraawa*, an olive garden, fenced round, in the middle of which there is a convent, and a subterraneous grotto. But by far the greatest interest is inspired by Jerusalem and the environs. In Bethany is the place where Lazarus was raised from the dead, and where the fathers still read a mass every year. On Mount Sion is the Cœnaculum, where Christ celebrated the Sacrament of the Lord's Supper with the apostles, washed their feet, appeared to the Ten after his resurrection, and eight days afterwards to St. Thomas; where St. Matthew was chosen an apostle ; where the Seven Deacons were appointed, and the first assemblies were held. Not far from it, in the Armenian Convent, is the place where Peter denied Christ, and then wept bitterly; and where our Saviour was a prisoner in the palace of the high priest. In the Valley of Jehosaphat, they shew the place where Christ parted from the disciples, to be alone with the three chosen ones—where he left the three to pray alone—where he sweated blood, and was betrayed by Judas. They shew, likewise, the footsteps on a stone under the bridge which crosses the Cedron, which are said to have arisen on the fall of our Saviour. In the church of the Holy Sepulchre, there are chapels in memory of Mount Calvary—of the grave of Christ—of the pillar where he was scourged—of the parting of his clothes—of the finding of the cross—of his appearance to Mary Magdalen under the figure of a gardener, and the stone on which his corpse was anointed. The place where our Saviour was crucified cannot now be ascertained. It is evident, from the accounts of the sacred writers, that it was at a short distance out of the city. It cannot have been on the spot which is now assigned to it, in the church of the Holy Sepulchre, for this is nearly in the middle of the present city, and can never have been outside of the walls.

North-east of it were the temples; north-west, the largest and finest palaces and residences of ancient Jerusalem; to the west, the city extended above a league, far beyond the walls of the present Jerusalem; to the south was Mount Acra, with its numerous edifices, and the buildings and market-places lying between that and Mount Sion. This difficulty was overlooked by those who, even in ancient times, affirmed, that Mount Calvary was under the present church of the Holy Sepulchre; that is, what was formerly nearly the middle of the city.

No objection can be made to the existence of the tomb of Christ on this spot. We know, that formerly sepulchres hewn in the rock, in the city, were common among the Hebrews. There can be no doubt, that this family vault was easily to be ascertained, and the place was certainly held in honour in the oldest times. The believers made pilgrimages to it, as the Jews were wont to visit the tombs of their relations. It is not improbable, that even in the apostolic age there was a kind of chapel there, which, being a place held sacred by the Christians, was treated by their enemies, as Eusebius describes, Vit. Const. III.25, 26. What unprejudiced person will fail to be interested by the simple narrative given by the father of ecclesiastical history of the building of the temple over the Holy Sepulchre, or who will think it doubtful? But in that place, Eusebius evidently speaks only of the Holy Sepulchre over which the church was built. Theodoret expressly distinguishes this from another church, which was built on the place where the cross stood, in Golgotha, and St. Cyril frequently assures us, that he had preached there. As these two places, both so important to Christians, were so often mentioned together, this may have caused them to be confounded after the destruction of the churches by Cosroes, when that in Golgotha wholly disappeared. This same place, or its immediate vicinity, is assigned by tradition, as the scene of many of the circumstances of the passion of our Saviour, for which, in consequence, particular chapels were destined. Mount Calvary was placed near it, in order to increase the interest of the series.

The Jews differ. from the Christians, in many respects, concerning the situation of places remarkable in Scripture. What the Christians call the Temple of Solomon, they call the School of Solomon. They place the temple rather more to the south, about where the *Sachara*, or temple of the presentation, is. The temple, they say, is in Moriah, which they also make the scene of Abraham's offering of his Son Isaac, which the Greeks, without reason, place on Mount Calvary. They place the tomb of David—of Solomon, and of other kings, on Mount Sion: but that of the prophets on the Mount of Olives, and the accuracy of the situation of the tomb of Jehosaphat, are not doubted. The seite of the other sacred places has been less disputed; and there is, in fact, no sufficient ground for contesting it. Whether there be an error of a few paces cannot be decided; but it would be ridiculous to think of disputing about it.

The Christians in Syria.

No province in the Ottoman empire has such a variety of Christian sects as Syria. The Catholics are of the Latin, Greek, Armenian, or Syrian church, or Maronites, and constitute almost a sixth part of the population of this province. The Latins, enjoy as Franks, certain privileges; the especial protection of the King of France, and other European princes, and form, both in political and religious affairs, a *status in statu.* But their privileges have been much abridged since the French invasion. Charles IV. King of Spain, applied in 1793, to Sultan Selim III. for the title of Protector of the Sanctuaries, or of the Fathers of the Holy Land. Napoleon, likewise, granted them this protection: but the applications made to the Divan in their favour were of no avail.

Divine service is performed by Franciscans, Capuchins, Carmelites, or Lazarists, who have been sent there from the convents in Europe. The first are, here, almost as ancient as their order, which appears, from the bulls of Gregory IX. of the 29th of January, 1230, and Alexander IV. of the 27th of March, 1257, in which the same absolution is given to them that had been received by the Crusaders. In the general chapter at Narbonne in 1260, the province of the Holy Land was declared to be the thirty-second, and divided into two guardianships, (custodia) of Cyprus and Syria. In 1291, they shared the melancholy fate of all other Christians in Syria; but since 1333 have been allowed to dwell at the Holy Sepulchre, and since 1342, to read mass there, and dwell in a convent on Mount Sion.

This convent they lost in 1569, and removed into the convent of St. John, then called St. Salvator, which they purchased from the Georgians, where they have remained to the present day, as in all the other convents belonging to this province, persecuted in various ways by the Turks, and continually at variance with the schismatic Greeks and Armenians about the sanctuaries. Besides the native Catholics of the Latin church, they include in their community the French subjects, who were formerly very numerous in Rama, Acre, and Saida; some kings of France, and lastly, Louis XV., in a diploma of 1725, declares the guardian of the convent of St. Salvator, apostolical commissary, and their subjects in those parts to be dependent on him in all ecclesiastical affairs.

These fathers still live at Jerusalem, where there are 800 Catholics belonging to their community; at St. John 80; at Bethlehem 100; at Nazareth 800; at Rama 2; at Jaffa 300; at Acre 80; at Arizza 2; at Damascus 200; at Tripoli 18; at Ladakia 20; at Aleppo 800; at Larnaca 600; at Cairo 700; and at Alexandria 2000; as superintendents of the churches belonging to their convents and in the sanctuaries of Jerusalem, Bethlehem, St. John, and Nazareth; as administrators and intercessors for Catholic Christendom, for which, and especially its princes, they read all the masses, and intercede for them in their prayers. They have been obliged to abandon the convents of Saida, Scandaroon, Rashid and Nicosia, for want of priests, but their convent at Constantinople is still inhabited by their commissary. The ecclesiastical affairs are managed by the guardians of the convent of Jerusalem, the economical by the procurator, and the whole collectively by the *Discretorium*. The Guardian is chosen by the Discretorium from those who have been missionaries or curators of the Italian nation, confirmed by the General of the order at Rome, and in the abovementioned parishes has almost all the authority of a bishop. The Procurator is chosen among the fathers of the Spanish, and the Vicar from those of the French nation. The Diseretorium is composed of these three, one priest of the Italian, and one of the German nation. Their disbursements, for the exactions of the Turks, for the maintenance of their churches and the poor, and their own wants, are defrayed from the alms which they used to receive from all the states in Christendom, but for the last forty years only from Spain, Portugal, and Italy. From the earliest times they have possessed considerable landed property. Thus they have many gardens in Jerusalem, which they let a long time ago to the Greeks, who at some future time will probably contest their right to them. Besides the olive-trees in the garden of Gethsemane, they had many others in the valley of Jehosaphat; but they lost these long ago, and by degrees many others, so that they have now only the few in the above mentioned garden. They pay annually to the pacha of Damascus seven thousand piasters, as ground-rent for the churches and convents in and near Jerusalem, and one thousand piasters for that at Damascus; to the pacha of Acre ten thousand piasters, as ground-rent for the churches at Nazareth, Acre, Saida, Naplous, Arissa, Ladakia, Tiberias, Naim, Tabor, Saphori, Jaffa, and Cana, which latter are however in ruins. They likewise pay from one thousand to two thousand piasters on the marriage of the governor or pacha, and other festivals. Since they have been deprived of the protection of the French minister at Constantinople, there has been

no end to the extraordinary demands made upon them. In
1805 the Pacha Abdallah demanded one hundred thousand
piasters; in 1806 a rather smaller sum; in 1807 one hundred
and forty-five thousand piasters, and in the following years
nearly as much. In 1813 he took only a hundred and seventy-
five purses, because he said he knew the bad condition of
Europe! Some years ago the procurator refused to satisfy the
demands of the pacha. It was immediately affirmed that he
had began to build in the convent of St. John, and a committee
of inquiry was sent thither, which cost him as much as the first
demand. The pacha frequently obliges them to purchase of
him cattle, fruit, and other things, at twenty times their value.
The arrival of the pacha of Damascus in Jerusalem every year
is like a day of judgment for the procurators of the different
convents. If he is dissatisfied with them, they are inevitably
visited with fine and imprisonment. Some years ago the
Mufti of Jerusalem required an annual tribute of one thousand
piasters. Eight years afterwards, when the fathers obtained
from Constantinople a firman, ordering the mufti to repay
these sums, he fled, besieged the city with some hundred peasants, till the fathers had given him the receipt, as if he had
paid the whole.

If one Christian party has had any repairs made in its church
or convent, the others immediately give information of it to the
Motsallem or Cadi, who never neglects such an opportunity
of imposing a fine. On the 18th of August, 1813, the governor
demanded two thousand piasters, on occasion of the birth of a
son of the sultan. The procurator refused, but three days afterwards was obliged to pay five thousand piasters, because a
child, which a servant of the Latin convent carried in his
arms, had a green branch in its hand. He was accused of
having violated the law. The opening of a third door in their
convent at Damascus cost them last year seven thousand
piasters, and they were forced to pay nearly as much this year
to retain the convent of St. John, where they were ill-treated
and kept prisoners for several weeks. The expences for the
poor Catholics in Judea also increased. Besides the dragoman and the servants of the convent, they have to support, according to established custom, the school-master and
all the children; all the widows and orphans; to keep in repair
the houses which fall to the convent for want of male heirs (in
the East women cannot inherit), without receiving any rent
from the occupants; to pay the annual land-tax for the Bethlemites; to supply in summer all the Christians with water from
their eight-and-twenty cisterns, while the other inhabitants of
Jerusalem purchase it of the Mahometans at ten para per

bottle; to maintain the poor, i. e. the greater part of the Catholics, and to furnish all Mahometans and Christians gratis with medicine from their laboratory. If a Catholic is imprisoned for any dispute or misdemeanour, they must redeem him; if not, the Greeks do it, and the delinquent goes over to their church. They have also to pay the other penalties for their poor brethren, which the Turks take care shall happen very often. This is particularly the case with the Bethlemites, who are almost every month engaged in disputes with the Motsallem of Jerusalem. Sometimes they had circulated false coin; sometimes they had not assisted a caravan, belonging to the Motsallem, when attacked by robbers; sometimes they all rise in a mass against the augmentation of the taxes for their fields. The fathers regularly pay one thousand piasters annually for this land belonging to the Catholics in Bethlehem, which has always been customary, on account of their great poverty. They do not perform any service for the fathers in return; they are even exempted from church dues, only on marriages, Twelfth-day, and Holy Thursday they make them presents of rosaries, crucifixes, or images of mother of pearl. The same may be said of all the parishioners belonging to the congregations of the fathers in the Holy Land. Here and there a custom has been retained from ancient times which is of advantage to them. Thus it is usual in Jerusalem for the superintendent to visit the grave of a deceased person three successive days after the burial, and he receives one piaster for each visit. Lastly, the maintenance of poor pilgrims from Europe, small as their number is, occasions them a considerable expence. Each has a month allowed him, during which he must be fed and taken care of in the several convents, where there are sanctuaries.

Thus these good fathers have laboured these thirty years under these manifold exactions. Their expences and debts increase; the latter already exceed 2,000,000 piasters; the number of their priests for missions is diminishing; within twenty years fifty of them have died, the majority of the plague; they will soon be obliged to give up other convents, and thus they gradually approach their entire dissolution. But it is said they have prepared their own misfortune: by pride, arrogance, scandalous publication of the sins made known to them by confession, by harsh treatment of their poor, and insolence to travellers, they have made themselves despised and hated, not only by the schismatics, but by their own brethren, and compelled them to labour at their overthrow. These reproaches are unhappily not entirely groundless. For want of good labourers, it has been necessary to admit bad ones into the vineyard of the Lord. The smaller number are true followers of Saint Francis, worthy to pray for Christendom at the tomb of their Lord ; many have done an injury to the good cause which can hardly be repaired.

When the French commercial houses and factories still flourished, the Catholics of the Latin church maintained a close connexion with them, carried on trade, and were very wealthy. In the French invasion they lost, like the French themselves, all their real property, and the greater part of them are now poor. In Jerusalem and St. John they live by the convent and by making rosaries ; in Bethlehem by that and agriculture. The situation of the Catholics in other cities is more tolerable. They call themselves Franks, and are recognized as such by the Turks, but they are all natives of the East; only a few of them understand Italian, and none of them Latin, in which language their divine service is performed. But they generally attend a sermon on Sundays and holidays, and when children, receive religious instruction in their own language, from the missionaries who have learned Arabic in the convents of Damascus or Aleppo. As the followers of Saint Francis have every where the cure of souls, the priests of other orders in Syria can be considered only as missionaries, for instance, the Capuchins at Damascus and Tripolis. It is only in Berout, and within these few years in Saida also, that they are priests of the Latin Christians. They too have always enjoyed the special protection of the kings of France.

The Carmelites have convents on Mount Carmel, in Tripolis, Bscherdi, and Aleppo, as also in Merdin, Bagdad, and Bassorah. The Lazarists have succeeded the Jesuits in Antura, Damascus, and Tripolis. Their situation is likewise very critical, as they receive no support from Europe, and the places of those who die are not filled up. In each of the above-mentioned convents there is but one priest. When Ghezzar Pacha, after besieging Acre, gave up to the discretion of the Mahometans the Christians and their property, the convent on Mount Carmel, which the French had changed into an hospital, was unroofed, as also its church, and the effects of the monks destroyed; since which time it has stood desolate. The monk intended for it lives in the hospital at Heifa, and visits it himself very seldom, but his servant does every day. Under Soliman Pacha the Christians were not allowed to go in pilgrimage to it. The convent has, however, been repaired, and considerable donations collected for it in France and Italy.

The Catholics of the Greek church are considered as pious, firm in their religion, and partly as martyrs. They have a patriarch, now Ignatius, who resides at Zug, in Kesrouan ; an

archbishop of Sur, now Cyrill Debas, who resides in his
diocese, and six bishops; for Palestine, Theodotion, Bishop of
Acre; for the Mount of the Druses, Basil, Bishop of Saida;
for Kesrouan, Theodotion, Bishop of Beirout; for Aleppo and
its environs, Basil, Bishop of Aleppo; for Damascus, Ignatius,
Bishop of Sacheleh; and for the Anti Lebanon, Clement,
Bishop of Balbec. Most of these bishops cannot visit their
dioceses, as their lives are in danger from the schismatic Greeks.
They have therefore their vicars, who make the episcopal
visitations in their stead, collect alms for the bishop, and
other purposes. They are chosen by the people among the
monks, as they must be unmarried, and a higher degree of
knowledge is expected from them; are instituted by the patriarch, and receive their confirmation from Rome. Their parish
priests, without any preparation, are also chosen by the people
and ordained by their bishop. This office descends from father
to son. I was assured that nothing more is required for it than
reading and writing, a knowledge of the ceremonies and of the
catechism, and some natural abilities. They perform the service and preach in Arabic, and have no notion of any other
language. Only the Bishop of Sur can live near his metro-
politan church, and visit his little diocese every year, in which
there are about two thousand Catholics and ten priests. The
diocese of Acre lies chiefly in Galilee, and has between four
and five thousand Catholics of the Greek church. The other
bishoprics are far more considerable. In Damascus there are
above ten thousand, and in Aleppo above fifteen thousand Catholics of the Greek church. They have always been exposed,
but particularly of late years, to the most violent persecutions
from the schismatic Greeks. Last year the patriarch at Damascus paid vast sums to the pacha to compel them to go over
to their church. They were obliged to pay great sums of
money, many were thrown into prison, and when they were
threatened with still more severe punishments, all the rich
members fled to Egypt, Lebanon, and Constantinople. Their
condition has probably been ameliorated on the arrival of a
new pacha, for this assurance was given them on their repeated
applications to the divan.

At Nazareth I was witness to an affecting scene with the
Bishop of Babylon. One Wednesday morning, early, the heads
of families of the Catholic Greek church, mostly venerable old
men, assembled in the Latin convent with their worthy priest,
an old man of seventy-five, at their head. They expressed
their joy at being able to pay their respects to a Latin bishop,
on which the speaker began to paint the melancholy prospect
they had before them, after the dreadful events in Damascus

and other places. He affirmed that they were ready to die as
martyrs for their religion, but they feared that hatred and persecution would not spare their families, and they therefore be-
sought the bishop to contribute to obtain some alleviation of
their fate, from the divan, by the intervention of the French
minister at Constantinople, which the bishop promised. The
tears which these venerable men shed were proofs of their
good disposition, and we parted with emotion.

There are no Catholic Armenians in Palestine, but their
number is considerable in Syria, and in Aleppo it amounts to
above 10,000. Their patriarch lives in Scharfi, on Mount Lebanon. They also are exposed to the most violent persecutions
from the Schismatics, which were very sanguinary at Constantinople in 1820, and the latter had there the triumph of
seeing four Catholic Armenian priests go over to them, most
scandalously betraying their own party. At Aleppo they have
frequently been called upon by the pacha to unite with the
Schismatics, and on their refusing to comply, he put many to
the torture, and ten were publicly beheaded; but even this
availed nothing. They remained firm to their church, many
fled, but most were ready to die for their religion. Hereupon
the persecutions ceased. So long as the Catholics of these
various churches are compelled to live with the Schismatics,
and to pay the extraordinary contributions to the schismatic
patriarchs, and are thus politically identified with them, their
lot will not be altered. Catholic Syrians are likewise only in
Aleppo and on Mount Lebanon, where their patriarch resides,
in a convent, three leagues from Antura; but they are very
numerous in Diarbekir. The few Catholics of the Chaldean
church in Aleppo are under their patriarch at Mohal.

Of all the Christian parties in Syria the Maronites are the
most numerous and powerful. They inhabit almost alone the
district of Kesrouan, and a great part of the Mountain of the
Druses. They have a patriarch, who resides at Kanowin, six
bishops, and six titular bishops. At Beirout and Trabolus
their community is more numerous than all the others together;
and in Aleppo, Damascus, Latakia, and Saida, they are also
very numerous. They reside likewise in several towns in
Palestine, and it is only about forty years since they withdrew
from Jerusalem. They are under the Bishop of Acre, and
their number is estimated at 200,000. All the Catholics of the
Latin church in Palestine, Syria, and Egypt, with the exception of the fathers of the Holy Land and their parishioners,
are under a bishop, now Gardolfi, of Piemont, who resides at
Antura in Kesrouan. He is at the same time the Pope's Legate

in these countries, and authorized to decide many disputes between Catholics of different churches, (which must otherwise be referred to Rome) and to give dispensations.

The other Christian Sects.

Next to the Catholics, the Greeks are the most numerous. They have two patriarchs, of Antioch and of Jerusalem, the former residing in Damascus, and the latter at Constantinople, where he administers the ecclesiastical affairs of all the Greeks, as the patriarch of Constantinople does their political concerns. He has a deputy at Jerusalem, an office which is now filled by the Bishop of Petra. Besides him there live at Jerusalem the Bishops of Nazareth, Lydda, Gaza, and Philadelphia; only the Bishop of Acre lives near his cathedral. The limits of their jurisdiction are not very strictly defined; those residing at Jerusalem are only titular, and serve to enhance the splendour of divine worship in Jerusalem in the eyes of the pilgrims who annually resort hither. The Greeks have at Jerusalem nine convents of monks and four of nuns, and four others in the vicinity. The monks of these convents, as of all others in Palestine, come from the Archipelago and other Greek provinces. Those among them are generally raised to the episcopal dignity who can pay the largest sum to the patriarch. The nuns also come here from distant parts, live here in a secluded manner as long as they please, generally for life, on alms and the produce of their needle-work; they pray the hours, like the monks, and wear a peculiar dress. According to long-established custom, contrary to the laws of the church, they are not for ever bound to the three vows. They also live on the alms which the monks collect, or which are left by the pilgrims in Jerusalem. The bishops, archimandrites, and many monks, live in the great monastery; in the others generally only one monk and some lay brothers; and in the nunnery from ten to twelve nuns; in the monastery of St. Saba, formerly so full, there are only ten, and in the rest from five to six monks. They perform all their prayers in the Greek language, which is the only one they understand. The country priests, however, are only acquainted with the Arabic, and their whole learning is limited to reading, writing, and a knowledge of the rites. The Greek churches are for the most part small, and all of one form.

The Greeks have in general an irreconcileable hatred towards the Catholics, place them on a footing with Turks and Jews, endeavour to persecute them in all possible ways, and,

on the other hand, to be on good terms with the other religious
parties, from which they differ in the dogmas as much as from
them.   At Jerusalem they sometimes approximate, receive
presents from each other, and the Greeks very artfully take
advantage of such opportunities to deprive the Latins of their
property in the Holy Land.   This hypocritical friendship pre-
ceded, for instance, the seizure of the garden of the Shepherds
at Bethlehem, as well as the entirely excluding them from the
Holy Sepulchre.   But those friendly relations were never of
long duration.

    It is very difficult to account for this hatred.   It is said to
arise from the difference in the articles of faith; but these are
not known either to their priests or the people, for they never
think of catechising or preaching; making the sign of the
cross, prostration before the reliques and images of the saints,
and observance of the fasts, are with them the main points.
For these they shew much more reverence than the common
people do among the Catholics.   First, they bow very low before the image, placed on a stone in the middle of the church,
representing the patron Saint; make three times the sign of
the cross—kiss it—make again the sign of the cross, and kiss
the ground : they then proceed to kiss all the images round the
church successively, and this is done by them all with as much
uniformity as if they had been trained to it from their youth
like soldiers.   Confession is general, and made by many at the
same time, with the observation that they have not committed
any of the sins enumerated the last time ; only when the sin-
ner is conscious of having committed a great transgression, he
confesses it to the priest in private, generally standing.   Among
the other Oriental Christians, both sit down together on the
ground.

    Nor is the difference of the articles of great importance, as
the Synods have long since decided.   The procession of the
Holy Ghost has been long understood and explained by
thinking Greek divines, according to the doctrine of all the
western churches.   The dispute respecting the validity of the
baptism of the Catholic church, on account of the form
Baptizo-te instead of *Baptizetur Servus tuus*, turns on a
logomachy, and it has been long since acknowledged to be
indifferent whether it is performed by immersion or aspersion.
But the repetition of baptism usual among them, in the case
of Christians of other sects joining their church, is condemned
by almost all Christian antiquity, and by several councils.   In
theory they deny purgatory, but in practice assume the forgiveness of mortal sin, by intercession in the mass, and require
large sums for it; at Jerusalem two hundred piasters for a

mass. In practice many adopt divorce, forgiveness of the sin of theft without satisfying the injured party, general confession, the attainment of salvation, without the knowledge of the articles of faith; but in theory they agree with the Catholic church. This antipathy appears therefore to be rather the work of the priests, who, whether from religious zeal or self-interest, hate the adherents of the Pope, whom they consider as the rival of their Patriarch. I know several Catholics who were induced by their fears to go with the French to Egypt. Being obliged, at the departure of the French, to return home to seek a livelihood, they arrived at Gaza, without provisions, without money, almost naked, and exhausted by the long journey through the desert. They crawled to the Greek church, hoping to obtain from Christians something to appease their hunger and thirst. They made themselves known; but when the Greeks heard that they were Franks, they replied to their intreaties that they might die like dogs, and that they were worse than the Mahometans. They did not like to apply to the Mahometans because they feared for their lives; but a Mahometan woman, who had observed them from her harem, saved them from inevitable death. She sent them meat and drink, and thus enabled them to continue their journey to Jaffa. National hatred too seems to have its effect: at least, the Moldavians, Wallachians, and Servians, though of the same religion as the Greeks, are their most inveterate enemies. But whatever may be the cause of their hatred towards the Franks in general, in Palestine interest is the chief motive. It is the contest for the possession of the holy places.

The Christians enjoyed for three hundred and fifty years the free exercise of their religion insured to them by Omar. Amurat interrupted it for a short time. But in 1009, the church of the Holy Sepulchre, which had been destroyed, was already rebuilt, and it appears from a decree of Muzafar, king of the Saracens, dated 1023, and from another of 1059, that the holy places were at that time confided to the care of Frank, i. e. of Catholic monks. This was likewise the case during the continuation of the sovereignty of the Frank kings in Jerusalem.

As soon after the crusades as the Holy Sepulchre was again accessible to the Christians, the disciples of St. Francis were the first who took possession of the holy places that had formerly been repaired and adorned by the Latins, prayed there, and being gradually assisted by pious contributions, especially of Robert, king of the Two Sicilies, and his wife Sancia, of Peter of Arragon, and of Jolm, king of the Two Castilles, they had in 1363 again fitted up all the sanctuaries and chapels for divine worship. The Sultan repeatedly confirmed them in the possession, and granted them firmans for their safety, in the years 1059, 1203, 1206, 1212, 1233, and 1407, which were expressly designed for that purpose, or tacitly in others, in which they received permission to build with lime, in the years 1203, 1213, 1271, 1310, 1397, 1411, 1446, 1495, 1501, 1502, and 1803; a permission which has always been purchased at a high price under the Mahometan governments. By degrees the other Christian sects took part in it, and soon began to contend with them for the sanctuaries, as is proved by the firmans of 1203, 1277, 1494, 1540, and 1558, which are directed against them, and secure the exclusive possession to the Latins. It was the Georgians especially who disputed the possession with them, and often combated with very powerful arms, because they were very rich. But when the alms from their own country failed, and could no longer pay tribute to the Turks, they were deprived of the possession, and succeeded in it by the Greeks, under whose protection they placed themselves. The latter, not satisfied with the chapels in the church of the Holy Sepulchre, deprived them in 1674 of the Holy Sepulchre and of the Stable (Præsepe) in Bethlehem, as well as the principal aisles of both churches. It was not till fifteen years afterwards that they restored both places to their rightful owners, on the intervention of the Emperor Leopold. But this only increased their hatred; and the firmans of various years, from 1540 to 1774, which the Latin fathers were compelled to beg from the Sultan by the intervention of France, and at times of Austria, sufficiently shew how violent and incessant the struggles of the two parties were. In those firmans the Sultan constantly repeats the form of words, " The Holy Land, and all that it contains, is ours by the right of conquest. The Latins have always possessed it as property purchased by them; it has always been confirmed to them as such, and therefore it cannot be taken from them—it belongs to them for ever." Though the words are so very precise, and but ill calculated to give another party hopes of acquiring this property, viz. the Church of the Holy Sepulchre, the Greeks did not lose their courage. On the 12th of October, 1808, a fire (whether arising from accident or design we will not decide) broke out in the church of the Holy Sepulchre, which consumed the whole of the upper part of it. The Greeks immediately hastened to Constantinople, and by paying large sums of money, of which the Divan was in need for the war against Russia, succeeded, in spite of the earnest remonstrances of the Latin commissioners, who, at that time, were destitute of the *nervus rerum gerendarum*, and of the protection of France, in obtaining the necessary firmans by which they alone were authorised to repair the church.

The Latins and Armenians strove in vain to join them ; they pre-tended they had all the necessary firmans to *build* the church ; but they had in fact only leave to make the necessary repairs, and while they were employed in procuring materials, the Pacha of Damascus came on a visit to Jerusalem. He being likewise bribed by them, interpreted the firmans as they wished, and they commenced their building with the destruction of all the Latin inscriptions in the whole church, and of all the sanctuaries, of the sepulchral monuments of Godfrey of Bouillon, and of Baldwin, and of two others, the monuments of Philip of Burgundy, and of Philip I. king of Spain, of the marble, with which the walls were covered, of the walls erected by St. Helena on the sacred rock, of the Mosaics of beautiful stones, of the sacred rock itself, and in short of every thing that even Cosroes had spared, in the presence of the Pacha, and erected upon the ruins the present church,-which they consider as their property. The procurator of the Latin convent protested in vain against these shocking acts of violence, against this horrible devastation. He was thrown into prison because he could not pay the sum of 50,000 Spanish dollars that was demanded of him. The Hattisheriff and counter orders which the French ambassador, M. de Latour Marbourg, obtained in 1811, came too late ; in consequence of this Hattisheriff, the Latins were going to replace their arms in the wall of a chapel formerly belonging to them, upon the spot where the cross is said to have been found. The Greeks would not permit this, alledging it was now their property. While they were employed in setting in a stone, a Latin father came to pray ; they struck him on the head with a hammer, and would have murdered him, had not his cries brought others to his assistance. The Greeks afterwards found out new contrivances to get possession of the Garden of the Shepherds, near Bethlehem, with forty olive trees, and to ill treat the catholic pilgrims who visited it. The Franks, without protection from France, which formerly secured them from such injustice, almost destitute of support from Europe, which would enable them to pay as large sums to the Turks as their adversaries, sink under this wicked de-ceit ; while the others can command the inexhaustible resources of their people, who spare no sacrifices, on the credit of the monks, under the pretext of saving the Holy Sepulchre and the sanctuaries from destruction, but in fact to outbid the Latins in bribing the Turks, and to expel them from Palestine ; and to put large sums of money into the hands of the Mahometans, their natural enemies, who know how to take advantage of their pride and their weakness. They always gain the victory ; they live with the Turks, are their dragomans, servants, and subjects ;

the Turks are always sure of their money; the Franks on the
contrary, are always aliens, always suspected by them, and
nothing but protection from Constantinople can preserve them
The Mahometans too, derive advantages from favouring the.
Greeks and Armenians, which the Franks can never afford
them. They have upon an average 4000 pilgrims annually.
The estimate of 38,000 Spanish dollars for the tribute called
ghafar, which they pay, is very low, and for this the pilgrims
have nothing more than the permission to visit the holy places.
The conveyance of persons and effects is chiefly in the hands of
the Mahometans, who possess the greatest number of mules
and camels; the profits arising from the consumption of provisions, &c. are shared between them and the Christians. To
this must be added, the extraordinary presents which the monks
themselves make at this time to the keepers of the church of
the Holy Sepulchre every time they open it, for the maintenance
of order, and to the Motsallem for the sacred fire. The ten or
twenty Latin pilgrims who annually visit Jerusalem, are almost
all poor, and provided with the necessary firmans. From
them, therefore, the Mahometans gain nothing. Of the small
sums, which the convent has to pay, the Pacha, the Motsallem, the Cadi, the Mufti, and the keepers of the Holy Sepulchre gain but little. It is, consequently, no wonder if the
Latins are oppressed and the others favoured.

The Armenians have in Jerusalem a patriarch, an archbishop,
about one hundred monks, and two hundred individuals of their
church. In Bethlehem, a convent with two monks, and two families; at Rama, a convent with one monk; at Jaffa, a convent
with three monks, and about fifty Christians of their sect. They
too frequently act in a hostile manner towards the Latins. Thus
the latter had formerly in the church at Bethlehem, a door
through the wall, which divides the principal aisle from the other
three parts of the cross. The Armenians closed it, and the Latins
remonstrated in vain against this violation of their rights, by
which they were cut off from the chief entrance to the sanctuary under ground. When during the French invasion no
doubt was entertained of the destruction of the Latin monks,
who were shut up with the catholic Christians in the church of
the Holy Sepulchre, the Armenians were the first to take possession of their chapels and valuable effects. But Sir Sydney
Smith, who came from Acre to Jerusalem, and hoisted his
standard on the Latin convent there, saved them and all their
property. A few years ago the Armenians made them offers
of peace, and of union with the Romish church. As a reward
they received the chapel near the spot where the cross is said
to have been found. But scarcely was the confirmation come

from Rome, when they separated again, still keeping the
chapel, which they have retained to this day. They are very
rich, and the alms which they receive seem to me to be more
considerable than those of all the other Christians.

The custom of giving alms to the Christians in Jerusalem is
very old. Even in the age of the apostles collections were
made for them among the other congregations, and we learn,
from Sozomenus and others, that it prevailed in later ages.
Charlemagne and many other princes were very liberal to them.
Henry VIII. in 1516, made a grant of two thousand pounds
annually to the Latins. In later times their chief patrons were
the kings of Spain, Portugal, and Naples, and the empress
Maria Theresa, who not only gave large sums and costly
utensils for the church, to the fathers of the Holy Land, but,
like all other Catholic princes, allowed alms to be collected for
them in their dominions, and thus millions flowed annually
from Europe to these convents. Since the second half of the
eighteenth century, the alms from many countries, as from
Austria and France, have failed; those from Italy have gradually decreased; and those from Spain and Portugal are
irregular.

The resources of the Greek and Armenian monks are now
far more considerable. They send agents all over the Turkish
and Russian empires, to collect for the poor Christians in Jerusalem, and to preserve the church of the Holy Sepulchre
from being destroyed by the Turks. The profit they derive
from the pilgrims is still greater. It is seldom that one of them
leaves Jerusalem without expending ten purses (seven hundred
and fourteen Spanish piasters), and the most spend two hundred
purses and more. The cunning monks contrive, under the
mask of piety, to get the last farthing from their pockets, and
it is known that many have not kept sufficient to pay the captain for their voyage home. The Muscovites were particularly
pillaged, and what the monks did not venture to do, was completed by the Turks. Earnest remonstrances were made; the
Greek patriarch repeatedly affirmed that he could not protect
them against the malice and insolence of the Turks, and thus
the Emperor of Russia found it necessary to establish a consulate at Jaffa for the protection of the pilgrims. This has had
the advantage, that many disorders have been prevented this
year; but it has increased the hatred of the Turks towards the
Muscovites. A Russian pilgrim has been murdered this year
at Tantura on his road to Jerusalem, by way of Jaffa; many
others have been very ill used and plundered at other places.
This establishment of a consulate may lead to another important measure, which would be likely to put down the in-

solence of the Greeks. The Russians demand a separate dwelling for their pilgrims; a convent for their clergy; and full power to celebrate mass in the holy places, according to the rites of their church. The Greeks will not grant them any of these points, and cannot do it without being great losers.

- The Christians in Syria have always been more exposed to the rapacity of the Mahometans than those in any other province of the Ottoman empire; and besides the usual oppression and ill-usage under which they have always laboured, they have been, in latter times, in danger of being entirely annihilated. So long ago as 1773, Abu Dahaw had conceived such a wicked project. The sultan threatened to depose him, because he had not for a long time sent him any money, and already owed him above five millions of piasters. But he came with an army to Syria, conquered Jaffa and Acre, from which Daher had fled with his treasures, and just as he was going to plunder and destroy the convents on Mount Carmel and at Nazareth, and to seize on the treasures of the temple in Jerusalem, he was seized with a severe illness, and died on the 10th of June, 1777. Tortured by remorse, he is said to have exclaimed, shortly before his death, " I have never done any harm to the Christians!"

After the retreat of the French, the Mahometans, under Ghezzar Pacha, were permitted to do as they pleased for three days with the Christians and their property. Many hundreds were killed or wounded, and almost all deprived of their property. Since that time the wounds have not been healed, and the tyranny of the Agas in the small towns falls chiefly on them. Formerly a Christian could abuse or strike a Mahometan, and was certain of being judged by the cadi according to equity. They were on more intimate terms together, and often forgot the difference of religion. Now the Mahometans look with haughtiness on the Christians; the slightest affront is attended with the most disagreeable consequences, and woe to the Christian who strikes a Mahometan. The Greeks are more intimate with the Mahometans than any of the other Christians, but do not on that account escape being ill-treated by them. The Catholics live entirely apart from them from their youth. I asked the Christians if the children did not sometimes play together? They replied, " Never, lest the children should learn the behaviour and bad language of the Mahometans." The Christian sects also live much apart from each other. The Maronites hardly allow Catholics of a different rite, and never schismatics and Mahometans, in their quarters. On the other hand, the Catholics find difficulty in settling in villages where none but schismatics reside. Their schools are always separate, and mixed marriages extremely rare. I was assured that the Catholic girls are extremely averse to schismatic men, and I was myself witness in a place where a poor but very handsome girl of the Latin church, refused to marry one of the richest Greeks in the town. An oppressive law obliges the Catholic Armenians to be married and buried by the schismatic priests, and to lodge with them on their pilgrimage to Jerusalem. It is seldom that any one goes over to another church. The Latin guardians of the convents of the Holy Land think it very meritorious when they bring back a Greek to their church. But here too interest has great influence. Among the Bethlemites there are many who would willingly become Catholics, if the convent would maintain them, and especially if it would pay their portion of the taxes. The Christians do not differ in their clothing from the Mahometans, only the latter generally have the turban white, striped with red, a shawl either party-coloured or green ; only the scherifs are allowed to wear the latter ; that of the Christians is usually blue, grey or black. The Franks alone have a right to wear a white turban ; the inhabitants of Bethlehem usurp it. The Jews wear a high cap, with a white and then a grey handkerchief round it, and a tuft of hair appears over the ears, which distinguishes them from the Christians. At Jerusalem the Christians cannot possess landed property. In other places they have lost it. In Nazareth they have a good deal, and in the Valley of Esdrelon, of which almost the fourth part belongs to the district of Nazareth, it is separated from that of the Mahometans.

All the Christians in the East agree in their strict fasts, when nothing of the animal kingdom is eaten with the blood warm, and all food dressed in oil. The clergy live on the alms of the congregation, and have no fixed income. There is much analogy in their mode of service. Preaching and catechizing are almost unknown to them. The mass, the prayers, and hymns, are said and sung so loud that all can understand them. Among the Greeks all join ; with the others the clergy sing and pray, and the people respond only at times. Only the Christians of the Latin church hear a sermon on Sundays and holidays. The smallest number perform divine service in their mother tongue ; the Latins in Latin, and only detached prayers, and in the mass the gospel, in Arabic ; the Greek monks all in Greek ; but the country clergy in Syria and Palestine all in Arabic ; the Maronites, and the Catholic and schismatic Syrians read mass in Syrian, but many prayers and the gospel in Arabic. The Catholic Greeks use in Syria and Palestine only the Arabic ; the Copts the Coptic and Arabic ; the Abyssinians the Ethiopian language.

There is a difference in the manner of fitting up their churches. In those of the schismatic Greeks the high altar is separated from the rest by a wooden partition. Those of the other sects are nearer to the form of the Latin churches. Forms and stools are unknown in the East; but in the richer churches there are carpets, upon which they sit on the ground in the eastern fashion. The churches of the Latins, Armenians, and Maronites are distinguished from the others by their cleanliness and cheerful appearance. All their churches are crowded with paintings, but the style is very different. The Latins have many good paintings, especially in Bethlehem, and in their other churches caricatures are rare. Those of the Greeks are still quite in the Byzantine style, without any variety, except those which have been sent them from Russia. Those of the Armenians have a peculiar style, quite different from the Byzantine. The figures are ill-shaped, but the countenances more agreeable, all after one model, with pale complexions, and bearing the characteristic features of their nation, among which the painter seeks his Christ, Holy Virgin, and saints. In the drapery they much resemble those of the Latins. The pictures of the Syrians in the main resemble the Byzantine, but are more imperfect. They frequently resemble strongly marked outlines more than finished pictures. At times you see among them some more like the Armenian. Those of the Copts bear the peculiar character of the national physiognomy; in other respects they much resemble the Byzantine school. The paintings are usually on wood; the Greeks alone employ gilding. There is nothing in the composition or execution of these paintings deserving of particular description.

I conclude these remarks with the wish that the condition of these Christians may be soon changed; especially that the indecent disputes in Jerusalem may speedily be terminated; that the documents may be again carefully examined; and each party recover what belongs to it. Many abuses must be remedied. The Latins set a good example: formerly the consecrated palmbranches were distributed on Palm Sunday in the church; this caused violent quarrels; it is now done in the court-yard of the convent. It must be established, that all the holy places occupied by the Turks shall be open without restriction and expence to the Christians, according to the conventions. Lastly, care must be taken that the Latins, as the possession of the most important sanctuaries belongs to them, and they represent the greatest number of Christians, be provided with worthy priests, who have before received a suitable education in the Propaganda, and, destitute of monastic pride, live solely for their duties. I mention as a model my friend Father Vito, who is esteemed and beloved by Turks and Christians.

Whether it would be advisable to send secular clergy thither may be reasonably doubted. The Turks are accustomed to the dress of these monks; they know that they are poor; the monks think it a point of honour in their order to preserve the Holy Land and the sanctuaries from total desolation. Secular priests may also fall into the faults above-mentioned. Pope Martin V. refused their petition to guard the Holy Sepulchre, instead of the Franciscans, and he confirmed this for ever in the Bull *Salutare Studium.*

The Festival of Easter at Jerusalem.

It is natural that the festival of Easter should be celebrated at Jerusalem with great solemnity. The pilgrims generally arrive from a week to four months before it, and return home immediately after. This year the several parties looked forward to it with a degree of apprehension, because it happened with them all at the same time, and each is then afraid of being ill-treated by the others. Each desires to have much time for the performance of the ceremonies, and contentions are unavoidable.

This year there was a most violent dispute respecting the grand procession in the evening of Good Friday. The Latins had hitherto been allowed four hours and a half for it. It was proposed that they should henceforth be limited to four hours. The Turks decided that the old custom should be retained. I attended the rites performed by all the parties, with exemplary patience, and cannot but lament that the Latins alone celebrate the festival in a manner worthy of the occasion. Even when we have made due allowance for the difference of the Oriental character, there is still so great a want of decorum in the manner in which the clergy behave at the ceremonies, in the rude and unnatural cries, especially of the Greeks, in the remaining in the church at night, in which many improprieties take place; and lasciviousness, especially at Christmas in Bethlehem, assumes an appearance of sanctity, in the holding a market in the church; in the most disagreeable deafening noise, continued often for hours together, which is produced by striking a long board hanging loose, or on a piece of metal, and in the crowding and fighting of the pilgrims, who, as it were, storm the chapels, as the poor do a baker's shop in a famine, that I was often determined never to attend them again. The most striking part of the ceremonies are their processions: and among the Latins the high mass, at which the guardian officiates with great dignity. The communion on Holy Thursday is very solemn. According to a custom, which has been retained from the primitive ages of Christianity, a quantity of provisions is brought by the Christians on this day, and distributed by the fathers among the poor.

It deserves to be noticed, that during the mass on Maundy Thursday, after the lessons have been sung, the Guardian kneels before the Holy Sepulchre, and with closed doors repeats a prayer, while very edifying hymns are sung in the choir. After the lapse of five minutes, the doors suddenly fly open. The singing of the mass on Maundy Thursday might be very moving, if they had but good voices. The procession on the evening of Good Friday, in which all the instruments, typifying the passion of Christ, are carried by different monks, is the most solemn. Sermons are preached at the same time, which refer to the passion or death of our Saviour.

If the most of the seven sermons in the seven principal chapels in the church, were delivered in the Arabic, and thus made generally useful, this would be a very good arrangement; but two in the Spanish language, which nobody understood, are useless, and four in Italian, by which few persons could profit, superfluous; that preached in Arabic by the Father Superior was listened to with great attention. The end of this procession is the signal for the processions and ceremonies, which continue through the night, of the Armenians, Syrians, Copts, and Greeks, which last, being by far the most numerous in clergy and pilgrims, make the most striking appearance. In the same manner the end of the high mass on Easter Eve is the signal for the most scandalous abuses of the church by the schismatic Christians, who conduct themselves in the most riotous manner. The Mahometan doorkeepers, and the Janissaries of the different convents, strike the good pilgrims on the head, face, and feet, at pleasure. They beat and throw each other on the ground, and run to the Sepulchre, all with the wildest cries. This is the preparation to receive the holy fire. At one o'clock the Motsallem of Jerusalem appears, and takes his usual place in the gallery of the Latins. At half-past one the Greek bishop, who is the deputy of the Patriarch, and called bishop of the holy fire, and who has the reputation of extraordinary piety, the procurator, and the Armenian bishop, go into the Holy Sepulchre, pray for half an hour with closed doors, then present the holy fire through the two lateral openings, to the pilgrims, who quickly distribute it all over the church by their wax tapers; and lastly, the Greek bishop carries it into the principal aisle, or division of the Greeks.

This year the Armenians had a violent dispute with the Greeks on account of the Syrian Bishop and the Coptic

Guardian, who also desired to be admitted into the chapel of the Holy Sepulchre, to receive the holy fire. The Greeks replied, that such innovations could not be allowed. Either the ancient custom must be observed, by which only the Armenian Bishop could be admitted to this honour, or else the later orders of the firmans must be followed, by which first the Greeks, and then the Armenians, were to receive the holy fire in the chapel. The Armenians, on their side, appealed to the Motsallem, and depending on forty Russian pilgrims of their church, threatened to complain to the Russian emperor. But the Russian consul rejected their appeal, and the Armenians said no more.

In the first ages of Christianity, it was customary for the Christians to pass the night of Good Friday in the church without light, and on the Saturday, to celebrate in common the whole service of the sabbath. When they went to rekindle their lamps, the patriarch, the clergy, the magistrates, and other Christians, made a procession to light the lamps of the Holy Sepulchre; the miraculous fire appeared; and this miracle is said to have continued till the taking of Jerusalem, by Godfrey of Bouillon.

In the 13th century, when the other Christian sects again assembled round the Holy Sepulchre, the Syrians and Abyssinians were the first who imitated this miraculous fire for the sake of the numerous pilgrims. Afterwards the Georgians shared the honour with them; and after their fall, the Greeks and Armenians undertook to receive the sacred fire in the chapel, and to distribute it to the other Christians.

The Catholics do not believe in the miraculous origin of it, but are of opinion that it is made by the Greek bishop, and is communicated very rapidly, because the wicks of the tapers given to the pilgrims are dipped in spirits of wine. The schismatic Christians are perfectly convinced of its supernatural origin and effects. Every one rubs himself with it; and it is sent by expresses to the churches in Jaffa, Acre, &c. The Greeks, Syrians, and Copts, conclude their pilgrimage by going to the Jordan to bathe. The Armenians for the most part content themselves with washing at Jerusalem, with water fetched from the river. The Latins have entirely discontinned this journey for many years, because they had many disagreeable scenes, and it generally happened that some of the monks were severely beaten. We set out on the 26th of April, accompanied by the Motsallem, with Turkish music. We met some caravans returning which set out the day before. Those which set out this day, about one thousand eight hundred persons, encamped in the plain of Jericho, and set out at two o'clock in the morning for the Jordan. Every one washed or bathed, but observed the strictest decorum ; filled · his bottle with water, and his pockets with pebbles from the bed of the Jordan. They then all returned cheerfully under the protection of the Motsallem, after paying the ghafar (tribute). At this year's festival of Easter there were one thousand four hundred Armenians, one thousand two hundred Greeks, thirty Georgians, three hundred Moscovites, sixty Copts, fifteen Syrians, one Abyssinian, twenty Oriental Catholics of the Greek and Armenian churches, four Maronites, and fifteen Franks.

The Ghafar.

The ghàfar is a tribute which the Mahometans think themselves entitled to demand of the Christians for permitting them, who are infidels, to pass through the countries belonging to the Faithful. This tribute is particularly introduced in Syria and Palestine, and in many places is so established by custom, that it is regarded as a legal tax, and he who attempts to evade it is in danger of being plundered or murdered. Only such Franks as have a firman from the Sultan, from the Pacha, or his Motsallem, declaring them free, are legally exempt from it. Most of them, by the intervention of their respective consuls, obtain from the Motsallem of Jaffa the necessary passports, one to the governor of Rama, from whom he receives another ; and one also for the entrance into the Holy Sepulchre.

Ghafar is paid for the first time on coming out of Egypt, in Arish, on the frontiers of Syria. When we rode by, the Sheiks did not venture to demand it of us, because we were recommended by Mahomet Ali Pacha ; they however asked for a present. Khan Jouness, the frontier town in Syria, is the second place where it is demanded. We appealed in vain to our firmans ; we were obliged to use force, and to repel, with arms in our hands, a swarm of Arabs who pursued us, and to put them to flight.

At Gaza, the only duty is upon merchandize. We paid nothing for our trunks, as they contained only our travelling equipage and no goods. At Jaffa six piasters must be paid, at Rama seven, at Kariataneb seven, at Jerusalem three ; and for the entrance into the Holy Sepulchre, twenty-three. Franks, without firmans, pay thirty-three piasters every time they go into this church ; one para for the entrance into the Holy Sepulchre; after the sacred fire, for the first few days, from one hundred and fifty purses to ten piasters, afterwards fifteen para; for the journey to the Jordan after Easter eighteen piasters; for the departure from Jerusalem, seven piasters ; in Kariataneb seven piasters ; in Rama seven ; before Jaffa three in

Jaffa, on departing, seven piasters. On the road from Acre by Nazareth and Nablous, you have to pay in Dschenin three piasters, in Nahlous seven, on departing three, in Suwije three, in Schafat seven, and in Jerusalem as above.

Besides this legal ghafar, a similar tribute is demanded by the Mahometans in many other places. On our journey from Jaffa to Jerusalem nobody ventured to demand it, because we were accompanied by a soldier of the Motsallem of Jaffa: for a large company it is advantageous to have such a one. The presents they expect are indeed great; but persons are then not exposed to be ill-treated by these privileged highway-men. The English pay it, though they are generally provided with firmans. This liberality, by which they also seek to get a good name among the Arabs, has done much injury to less opulent travellers; for my part I never paid it. In Dschenin, and in Nablous, I got rid of the demand, by appealing to my firman. On my departure from the latter place they at-tempted to compel me ; but I hastened to Ibrahim, the go-vernor, who on reading the firman, dismissed me with kindness, and declared me exempt from payment. But the most dan-gerous adventure in this respect occurred at Suwije. On en-tering the narrow valley, on the right hand of which this nest lies, four fellows, armed with stones, lay in wait for me, and threatened to kill me if I did not immediately give up my property. I replied that I travelled under the protection of the Pachas of Acre and Damascus, and of the Motsallem of Na-blous, but all was in vain ; they seized my horse's bridle, I drove them off with my pistols; they stoned it—I was forced to submit to this for fear the other inhabitants of the village, to whom they cried for assistance, should come up ; besides, it rained so hard, and my whole body was so benumbed, that I was scarcely able to urge my horse forwards. They were at last tired of waiting in this bad weather, and contented them-selves with a trifle which my guide gave them But he had scarcely got rid of them, when another came up and demanded the ghafar. I gave him a peremptory refusal. He threatened and demanded my firmans. This I refused, as I knew before-hand that he would tear them. These robbers have often done this, even with firmans from the Sultan, which the other Arabs always regard with the greatest respect. He called for help, but no one came except the four banditti. It now suddenly began to thunder and lighten, and the rain increased, which made them all retire. At the end of this valley, which is two leagues in length, another Arab was sitting with his musket in his hand, and two others were seen at a distance. He demanded the ghafar, if we were bound to pay it, for he had a right to ask it; but nobody answered him, upon which he arose and threatened us. Upon this two Sheiks, who by this time had joined us, replied that he had nothing to claim; that they were inhabitants of the country, and good Mussel-men; but that I was a Hend (Indian). He then quietly sat down again; the storm increased; and I believe that all these people knew of my coming, otherwise they would certainly not have exposed themselves to the inclemency of the weather. In Sendschel no demand was made. I went into the house of a Greek, the only Christian in this great village. I here dried my clothes, which were quite wet, and warmed myself at the fire. On the following day I travelled without any in-terruption, for nobody met me on this interesting road. It was not till I, arrived near Schafat, that I saw four fellows hasten towards me, who I feared intended to plunder us. I pointed out the danger to my mule-driver, and ordered him to drive quickly, but our mules were obstinate and the danger was too near. Before they came up to us, they raised a great cry, and commanded us to stop, which we did not do. They approached us, armed with muskets, swords, and pistols. I was extremely alarmed, remote from all assistance, not a soul near, not a village, except the one half a league distant, from which these robbers came. I renounced all hope of saving my life. They commenced with disarming my mule-driver, and beat him severely. They seized my bridle and threatened me with their sabres if I made any resistance. I appealed to my firmans, entreated; promised them presents, but all in vain, and they conducted us to the neighbouring village. We could not obtain an explanation of their conduct; they took it for granted that we knew the reason of it. They only affirmed that they were right, we were impostors, they acted openly, and we tried secretly to evade the laws. We at last arrived at the vil-lage, where I met with an Albanian, a soldier of the Motsaliem of Jerusalem, whom I immediately requested to protect me against these robbers. He encouraged me and said he would accompany me. We then proceeded to the second part of the village, situated on the main road from Nablous to Jerusalem, where there is a toll-house. My Arabians first entered the apartment, round which, five and thirty Arabs were sitting engaged in earnest conversation. They here accused me of having left the high road to avoid the toll-house, and not pay the tribute. They had run after me they said, and delivered me to justice. It is true, I said, I had a firman, but this they did not believe, for, in that case, I should not have secretly left the main road. They all looked at me, and I replied that it was untrue that I had intended to

evade a legal tribute; that I was ignorant of this road, as well
as of the toll-house; that they were equally unknown to my
mule-driver, who had never made this journey but once, and
not in the main road ; he had therefore been unjustly beaten.
I stated that I had desired him to conduct me to some ruins,
and that he had done so, and contented himself with bringing
me on the way to Jerusalem, but not into the main road which
we had followed before; that I was a Frank, and had therefore
to pay no tribute, and had besides been dispensed from it by a
firman. Upon this I gave my firman to the Sheik, who had it
read aloud. They now treated me with great civility, pronounced me free of the ghafar, and begged me to tell the Motsallem of Jerusalem, that I had been with them, and had been
very well received. I now, at length, comprehended the
meaning of all the expressions which had before so much
alarmed me, when they repeatedly affirmed that we were
cheats; they looked upon us in the same light as many Christians and Jews who go far about to avoid this toll-house, where
every one has to pay seven piasters. A short time before the
attack, we met a Jew, who, doubtless, evaded it, and was
pleased to meet with companions.

The Inhabitants of Palestine. Towns and Villages in the
Pachalik of Acre, and the District of Nablous and Kuddes.

Syria was formerly divided into the five Pachaliks of Aleppo,
Damascus, Trabolus, Saida, and Gaza. Daher took from
the Pacha of Saida the land of the Druses, and also the whole
coast from Nahr el Kelb to Carmel, and confined him to Saida,
from which he likewise expelled him in the sequel. After the
fall of Daher, Ghezzar Pacha restored the ancient Pachalik,
united to it Safad, Tiberias, Balbeck, and Cæsarea, took Beirout from the Maronites, and transferred his residence to Acre.
Afterwards, Jaffa, Gaza, Rama, and Nazareth, were annexed
to it, and on the appointment of Abdallah, Pacha of Tripolis,
to the dignity of Pacha of Acre, the Pachalik of Tripolis,
where the mountain chain on the Orontes forms the frontier,
so that the Pachalik of Acre is now one of the largest and
richest in the Turkish empire. The Pacha annually pays to
Constantinople, about two millions of Turkish piasters, besides the presents which he has to make to his patrons in the
divan. The rest of Palestine fell to the Pacha of Damascus,
under whom it still is, though the Christians are very desirous
of having one Pacha of Palestine, and have petitioned to that
effect at Constantinople, hoping that this would prove a check
on the ill-treatment and extortion to which they were exposed.

They always received for answer, that the Pacha of Damascus had need of the revenues of this city to defray the expences of the caravans with provisions, which always go to meet the pilgrims on their return from Mecca. The last Pacha had been recalled towards the beginning of 1821. His place was supplied by a late Grand Vizier. At the time of my leaving Syria, it was generally affirmed that he had brought two great men from Constantinople with him, 'one of whom was intended for Pacha of Acre, and that Abdallah had fallen into disgrace because he did not send enough money to the divan.

Abdallah is devout, not without talents, but guided by counsellors, who, under the pretext of religion, endeavour to do all possible injury to persons who are not of the Mahometan religion. It was by their influence that Hajim, his powerful minister, a Jew, was strangled on the 24th of August, 1820. This able statesman, for twenty years sole minister in Acre, lost one eye through Soliman Pacha, on his pilgrimage to Mecca, and as the latter owed the Pachalik to him, he also, by his great credit, got Abdallah, Pacha of Tripolis, to be appointed Pacha of Acre. One of his brothers is equally powerful, who is minister to the Pacha of Damascus, their native city. A third brother is first secretary to the Reis Effendi at Constantinople. The Pachalik of Acre enjoys this advantage over others, that its Pacha generally holds his place for life, while most of the others retain it for only one year, which time is often prolonged, but often abridged. Abdallah endeavours to show his love of justice by returning their lands to those who lost them under Ghezzar, especially during the French invasion. But he indemnifies himself tenfold, by seizing the possessions of the little Emirs or Sheiks on the mountain of the Druses, who were hitherto independent or only tributary. Three of them have already become the victims of his tyranny, and great fermentation on both sides of Lebanon is the consequence. Who knows whether the liberty which these good mountaineers have preserved for centuries, may not be destroyed by these events? Twenty years ago they were deprived of Beirout, their sea-port, by the despotic Ghezzar, and now their very vitals are attacked. The consequences to the Christians in Syria, who, in times of persecution, always found a refuge in the mountain, are incalculable. But, however cowardly they may appear to have become, danger will unite them; the fire kindled in the spring of 1821, will spread through Lebanon and defy the pretensions of the tyrant of Acre, if he should continue to demand more tribute than their ancestors paid, to destroy institutions which centuries have sanctioned, or should he attempt to deprive them of their arms, which the Orientals

regard as their greatest treasures. When I visited Lebanon,
the fermentation was greater than ever. The treasurer had fled
with large sums, which he had extorted from the Maronites and
Druses in the name of the Pacha, who now required them to pay
these extraordinary contributions over again, which they were
unable to do. A body of troops, stationed at Saida, was to terrify them, but it was in vain. At the beginning of May all the
Christians in Syria were disarmed.

The number of inhabitants in Kesrouan, is estimated at
200,000, and on the mountain of the Druses, at 160,000. The
whole coast from Khan Jouness, to Nahr el Kelb, and also
Trabolus and Latakia, and the whole of Galilee, is the property of the Pacha; it contains the towns of Gaza, Jaffa, Acre,
Tiberias, Sur, Saida, Beirout, Tripolis, and Latakia.

Gaza lies in a very fruitful tract, a quarter of a league from
the sea. Olives, figs, oranges, &c. grow in abundance; the
houses are chiefly built of hewn stones, the remnants of ancient
buildings, and are very low, so that the town covers a great
extent of ground in proportion to the number of the inhabitants,
which is only six thousand, all Mahometans, except three
hundred schismatic Greeks. The streets are narrow, unpaved,
and crooked. There is a good deal of communication in the
town, from the trade by land between Egypt and Syria, the
goods being conveyed by camels, of which many of the inhabitants have large herds.

Jaffa is on the sea side, and has a port, which is, however,
very unsafe, and in winter dangerous. The town is small,
situated on an eminence which commands the whole surrounding country. The only broad street is that next the sea, in
which are the Bazars, which are much richer than those of
Gaza. There is a considerable trade into the interior of Palestine, but there are seldom more than ten vessels here in summer,
and in winter none. Only just after Easter the number is
greater. The English have a vice-consul, the Austrians and
Germans an agent, both of Jaffa, the Russians a consul, who
has been appointed within these twelve months, chiefly on account of the pilgrims. The affairs of the French, Spaniards,
and Italians, are managed by the procurator of the convent
of the Holy Land. There are about three hundred Christians
of the Latin, and three hundred and fifty of the Greek church,
and three thousand Mahometans in Jaffa.

Rama is in a very fruitful plain four leagues from the sea.
No city in Syria has suffered more from the French invasion
than Rama. There were several French factories, which had
almost the exclusive trade with manufactured goods to Gaza,
Jerusalem, and Nahlous. Now only one monk resides in the

hospital of the fathers of the Holy Land. All the other Christians of the Latin church have either been murdered, or have lost their property and fled to Jaffa, Jerusalem, or Acre. The Greeks are above five hundred.

Acre is the residence of the Pacha of the whole coast of Syria. It lies on the sea, in a fertile but almost uncultivated plain, three or four leagues broad. The harbour is protected from the west and north-west winds by some houses built on rocks in the sea ; but it is small, and choaked with sand, so that it is fit only for a few small vessels : the others lie at Haifa. All the streets of Acre are narrow, ill paved, and dark, except the bazar. The houses are ill built. The town is surrounded with a wall and ditch, and having only one gate, it is easy to take note of those who come in and go out. No strangers can enter till application has been made to the Pacha for permission, for which they generally have to wait an hour at the gate. There are four richly furnished bazars, the handsomest of which is near the Pacha's residence ; it was built by his predecessor. It is intended to add a large khan, and the houses have been already pulled down, and the work commenced. Acre has from 12 to 15,000 inhabitants. The great majority are Mahometans, and have four mosques, one of which, lately finished, is among the handsomest in the Turkish empire. A magnificent bath, and a library, are attached to it.

Opposite to it is the residence of the Pacha, an irregular building, of which the harem is, as usual, the handsomest part. Cannon are planted in the court-yard, and it has a garden, the only one in this small and crowded town. The other inhabitants are, 800 Greek Catholics, 80 Latins, 800 schismatic Greeks, 80 Maronites, and 800 Jews. Each of the Christian communities has a church. The Latins, besides their parish church, which is a neat plain edifice, near the sea, have a chapel in their convent, and had formerly a very handsome little church, with marble walls and pillars; but, because it was higher than other buildings, Soliman Pacha ordered the roof to be taken off, in spite of the remonstrances of the French consul, who used it as his private chapel. It now lies in ruins. The church of the schismatic Greeks is the largest, and near the convent, where their bishop resides.

Almost the whole trade is in the hands of the Pacha and of the Austrian consul, who is also Russian vice-consul. They are owners of several ships : they purchase the oil of Samaria and the cotton of Galilee for exportation, and sell, on the other hand, manufactures in the country.

The chief trade of Palestine is with Egypt. Above two hundred vessels arrive from that country annually at Jaffa, and still more at Acre, laden with rice, linen, sugar, some fruits, and manufactures. Palestine exports, oil, olives, cotton, tobacco, pipe-heads, earthenware, soap, and, in productive seasons, corn. The soap manufactories are numerous, and the soap much celebrated on account of the good potashes obtained from the plants of Arabia.

The difference in the kinds of money current in the Turkish empire, is a great impediment to commerce. . For a Spanish dollar you receive in Egypt twelve piasters; in Jerusalem, seven and a half; in the sea ports, from Gaza to Acre, eight; from Sur to Trabolus, eight and a half; in the rest of Turkey, seven piasters. The great difference arises from their coining in Egypt piasters which are not equal in value to other Turkish piasters (properly an ideal coin). European gold always loses considerably in Turkey.

Nazareth is at the foot of a declivity, between mountains from north to south: the streets are crooked, the houses low, chiefly of stone: there is a Latin convent, four churches, and one mosque. No Jews are ever allowed to show themselves here. The convent is the cleanest and richest in the Holy Land, possessing gardens, lands, and houses, with shops. Each of these shops is let for two piasters; the Pacha demands four for his. Some applicants, willing to outbid each other, having offered four to the fathers also, the guardian answered " *La Madonna no vuol piu*"—(The virgin will have no more.) Many old men so related to me, with emotion, this simple answer. The church is spacious, and tastefully decorated. It consists of three parts; the church itself, in which there are seven altars, and paintings of subjects taken from scripture; the sanctuary, to which you descend by seventeen steps, and the choir of the fathers over it, with stairs to each side of the entrance into the sanctuary. The Latins are about 800; the schismatic Greeks 1200. Their church was built about seventy years ago, in the usual Greek form. Formerly, they had no church at Nazareth, till they obtained permission to build one, through the intercession of the Latins: but they were obliged to erect it 200 paces from the town. The Catholic Greeks, 200 in number, performed divine service in a church belonging to the Latins. The Maronites, 250 in number, have a church of their own. The Mahometans are under 300, and their mosque lately built. The whole amount of the inhabitants is 3000.

Tiberias, on the west bank of the sea of Galilee, is surrounded with walls; the houses are for the most part miserable huts, excepting the castle, the residence of the Motsallem, and the new house of the former Austrian consul at Aleppo, who is resolved to spend the rest of his days here. The inhabitants are partly Greek Catholics (about 300), partly Turks, and partly Jews, chiefly foreigners, especially Poles, who almost all live on alms. I was moved with pity when I walked about the quarter of the Jews. Ragged figures, in dirty, wretched, half ruined houses, are now the only population of this spot, which was once the resort of many thousand students. I visited the synagogue of the German Jews, which I found, though in a better condition than that of the Oriental Jews, 'like it, empty, without any ornament, and but a few books on the benches. I saw the synagogue of the Portuguese, which is rather larger and handsomer, and may be best compared with ours in Europe. I examined their libraries, and besides some MSS. of the fifteenth century, found only Hebrew and Rabbinical books, printed in Italy, Germany, Amsterdam, Lisbon, and Constantinople, which had been brought by the Jews. The children and adults were employed in some schools in learning the elements of reading and writing, in others with the Talmud.

Sur is a little walled town on the sea, but its port is not much frequented. The country next the town is sandy, and it is about a quarter of a league to the east that the celebrated fertile tract commences. The inhabitants are three thousand, including one thousand five hundred Catholic Greeks, with an archbishop, and three hundred schismatics. Each of these two parties has a church; that of the Catholics is large, and simply ornamented.

Saida, formerly the residence of the Pacha, has lofty walls on the land side. The harbour, like most of the others, is choaked up with sand. The bazar is extensive, and though Saida has lost much by the removal of the Pacha's residence to Acre, it is still very lively, because part of the trade from the mountain of the Druses passes through it. Formerly there were many French commercial houses, of which only two remain. The inhabitants are chiefly Mahometans. The whole number is eight thousand, including five hundred Greek Catholics, four hundred and fifty Maronites, four hundred schismatic Greeks, and eighty Jews.

Beirout lies on a plain ; the harbour is sandy and small, but there is a large bay a league to the north, to which ships resort. There are in the neighbourhood many gardens, planted with vines and mulberry-trees. At a distance are groves of fir-trees, which are said greatly to improve the otherwise bad air. The town is extensive; the bazar large and rich. It is well situated for trade; that of Damascus, the Kesrouan, and the mountain of the Druses, being chiefly carried on through it. It has about ten thousand inhabitants, of whom four thousand are Turks; almost all the rest Maronites, except about fifty Franks, one hundred Jews, some schismatic and Catholic Greeks, and a good many Druses. About five thousand people daily come from the mountain to the city to trade. The Austrians have a consul, who is also Russian consul; the French and English each an agent.

Tripolis lies on the sea; has eight thousand inhabitants, chiefly Maronites, one hundred Franks, several convents and consuls. It is not so well situated for trade, yet it is more lively than Latakia, through which the greater part of the traffic from the sea to Aleppo is carried on.

Each of these cities has a Motsallem, or governor, appointed by the Pacha of Acre, and generally changed every year; a commander of the garrison, consisting in Nazareth, Tiberias, and Sur, of fifty men; in Acre, of four hundred; and in the others, of two hundred men. Receivers of the taxes are appointed out of the different religious parties, who pay them to the secretary of the Motsallem. The taxes are levied on the male inhabitants above twelve years of age, according to their ability, from thirty to three hundred Turkish piasters. These regular and pretty equitably distributed taxes, are less burthensome than the extraordinary imposts on the birth of the Sultan, his marriages, the marriage of the Pacha, &c., the amount of which is fixed by the Pacha. The towns, which have gates and walls, (all except Gaza and Nazareth) are shut up at night, and the keys carried to the governor, without whose permission the gates cannot be opened.

In each city there is also a cadi, sent from Constantinople, who administers justice in the town and neighbourhood.

These Motsallems have under them the villages in the plain between the Mediterranean and the territory of the Pacha of Damascus, the desert of Arabia, the mountains of Halil, Kuddes, Nablous, and the Jordan, the sea of Galilee, and some villages on the sea between Sur and Beirout, Trabolus, and Mintaburg. They are mostly small, inhabited by from twenty to three hundred families, who chiefly subsist by agriculture and breeding cattle. The houses are chiefly built of black earth, in the form of a cone, very small, and so low that one must creep into them. The inhabitants are in general very poor; the women in blue shifts, with a handkerchief on the head falling down behind. The men miserably clothed, but in different fashions and colours. The long Oriental dress is seen every where, but only worn by the rich. In the fine vallies of Galilee I saw many tents of the Arabs, who feed their horses on those luxuriant but uncultivated fields.

The dirt, the vermin, and the smoke, make their houses extremely disagreeable, and I have often been obliged to repulse the good-natured importunity of the Arabs. In the towns the houses are chiefly of stone, one story high, with many apartments. In the principal towns, as Acre, Jerusalem, and Nablous, there are also large houses, with seats on both sides of the entrance, a court-yard with a piazza round it, several rooms, and a handsome division for the harem. Many dwellings are made in some villages in the caves of the mountains, which are particularly numerous in Judea.

The population of all Syria may be estimated at three millions. It appears less because the villages and towns are not considerable, the statements given by the inhabitants low, and the sum paid for the poll-tax small. But when we consider that twenty or more persons often sleep in a small hut; that the inhabitants generally count only the males, and therefore the women and children must be added ; and that the poll-tax is paid only by males between the age of twelve and fifty years, our estimate will not be thought too high. The Pachalick contains perhaps a third of the above-mentioned number.

The ten villages on the mountains between Halil and Rama, have also lately become tributary to the Pacha of Acre. The men of these villages, amounting to about three thousand, are robust, warlike, savage, rapacious, and always armed. Fifty years ago they could with impunity defeat and kill the Pacha of Damascus, who attempted to subdue them with an army. At that time they were allied with many other villages between Halil and Gaza; but the latter have since been gradually subdued by the Motsallem of Gaza; yet they continued to make war on the Motsallem of Jaffa, and to attack every year the inhabitants of the plain, till a few years ago, when their Sheik Elazasi, generally residing in Talsafi, was made prisoner. He was kept half a prisoner at Acre, till Abdallah Pacha released him about a year ago, with a present of some clothes, at the request of Abugos, the chief of another tribe, who was formerly at war with them, but is now become their friend, and on the promise of the Sheik that the villages should remain tranquil.

In the same manner the villages under Abugos are likewise bound in some degree to the Pacha of Acre. The country is in the middle between Jerusalem and Rama, and the chief seat is Kariataneb (St. Jeremiah.) This Sheik is less powerful by the number of his subjects than by the advantageous position of his territory among mountains. Most of the places are built on mountains that are nearly inaccessible. This tribe is notorious for its ill treatment of the Christian pilgrims and the Jews. The road from Jaffa to Jerusalem passes by Kariataneb, the chief seat of these privileged banditti, which no pilgrim ventures to avoid without exposing himself to the greatest ill-usage, and indeed cannot well avoid, on account of the steep mountains. There he has to pay seven piasters for himself, and two for his baggage. This toll or ghafar is according to their language legal.. Hundreds who were unable to pay, have been here wounded or even murdered. The convents at ·Jerusalem are especial objects of their extortion. Besides the usual payment that they have to make Abugos for suffering their pilgrims and provisions to pass, he daily makes new demands on them. He pays annually to the Pacha of Acre from thirty to forty purses (five hundred Turkish piasters each); to the pacha of Damascus, forty purses, and large presents to the governors of Jerusalem and Jaffa, and to several Sheiks in Jericho on the east bank of the Jordan, and others.

Though his revenue is large (above ninety thousand piasters), he affirms that he has little left for himself, being obliged to make large presents of shawls, horses, &c. to those who aid him in his robberies. He is intimately connected with the Sheiks on the Dead Sea and the Jordan, without whose assent he never begins war. So long as the old Abugos lived (he died three years ago, of the effects of a long imprisonment at Acre), their affairs went on well, but they are much dissatisfied with the present chief, because he is covetous, and does not share his booty with the others. He has two brothers. It has been observed that no chief of this family has died a natural death. Three years ago he had the misfortune to lose one of his sons, who was cut to pieces by the inhabitants of a neighbour-ing village. At the beginning of April, 1821, he conquered the village, and killed many of the inhabitants. Sir Sydney Smith sent him a handsome pair of pistols, a dagger, and some printed leaves of the Koran. The late Queen of England, then Princess of Wales, made him presents of the value of twenty-one thou-sand piasters. He is also fond of making presents, but people do not like to receive them, because they are obliged to make him presents of twice the value in return.

This banditti chief is esteemed, because he is powerful, keeps his word, and his protection and assistance may be de-pended upon; whereas the legal governors murder and rob under the cloak of the law, and these districts are a scene of plunder and robbery when a Motsallem or a Pacha dies. We were in danger from such troubles, when the inhabitants of Nahlous were in a state of insurrection in February, 1821, and all Palestine was for a few days in arms.

Before the French invasion these tribes were involved in continual feuds, the consequence of which was, the desolation of the country, the extinction of many chief families, the de·

struction of the villages, and the ruin of the inhabitants; till
about twenty years ago the Pacha of Damascus, by his vigo-
rous measures, inspired terror into all these parties, so that
a traveller can now go, on payment of the ghafar, from Rama
to Jerusalem, and when he visits the Dead Sea and the Jordan,
may hope to escape without being murdered or plundered, if
he has some soldiers of the Motsallem of Jerusalem to protect
him; but this journey should never be undertaken without
such an escort, as several Franks, who thought they could dis-
pense with it, have experienced.

The ancient Samaria is now mostly under the Pacha of Damascus; though the country is mountainous it is well peopled.
One hundred villages belong to the district of Nabolosa, the
governor residing in Nahlous, a large town said to contain
three times as many inhabitants as Acre.   They are said to
be malicious and thievish; but I was exposed to less danger
than at Dschenin, where they wanted to show me how they
cut off people's heads; whereas here I was only stared at, and
questioned about my country and my religion.   The priest of
the schismatic Greek church too, assured me they were not so
bad as they were represented.   The streets are broader and
cleaner than in other Arab towns, and I nowhere saw so many
houses, with Arab sentences from the Koran inscribed over the
doors in red letters, which distinguish the houses of those who
have made the pilgrimage to Mecca.

Jerusalem.

Jerusalem has about eighteen thousand inhabitants, viz. eight
hundred Christians of the Latin church, eleven hundred of the
Greek, two hundred of the Armenian, and fifty of the Coptic
and Syriac; the number of the latter diminishes while that of the
Armenians increase; five thousand Mahometans, and ten thousand Jews.   The number of the latter increases annually; it is
said that five hundred often come from Europe in one year, and
hardly fifty go away.   Only the foreign Jews are rich; those
born here live on alms sent from Europe by their rich brethren.
The city lies on an irregular eminence, and has six gates.   The
church of the Holy Sepulchre belongs to the Greeks, Latins,
Armenians, and Copts.   The building was commenced by the
Bishop Macarius, under Constantine, and completed by
Maximus.   It was repaired by Heraclius, and subsequently
often destroyed and rebuilt.   Each of the Christian parties has
its own chapel for divine worship, and dwellings for the
monks, who pray there day and night.   Four Turks are there
as superintendants, and as they often have friends with them,
you sometimes see twenty Mahometans sitting on the divan at

the door, or striking with their whips the poor pilgrims in the church. They never open the church but in the presence of a dragoman of the Greek, Latin, and Armenian convents. Each pilgrim pays twenty-three piasters the first time he enters, and afterwards one para each time.

The church of St. Salvator is in the Latin convent, and the only one belonging to the Franks. Almost all the Greek clergy are united in the great Greek convent, where five bishops, six archimandrites, the procurator, and fifty monks and deacons reside. They have their board and lodging, one hundred piasters annual salary, and five thousand piasters for masses. They have to reside almost the whole year in the convent, to attend the ceremonies for the pilgrims, and add to the splendour of them. This convent contains the church of St. Constantine and St. Helena, which is full of paintings, and possesses many relics. It joins the church of the Holy Sepulchre. The Greeks have several other churches in Jerusalem, viz. those of St. Demetrius, of St. Nicholas, of St. George, (with an hospital for the aged and infirm), of St. Michael, of St. Basil, of the Holy Virgin, founded by St. Milasia, of St. Euthymius, of St. John the Baptist, of Abraham, of St. Maria Egyptiaca, containing a very ancient picture of the Virgin, and of St. James.

The Armenians have undoubtedly the finest convent in Jerusalem, formerly belonging to the Georgians, who were obliged to leave it because they were unable to make the customary presents to the Turks. The Armenians obtained it by presents in spite of the remonstrances of the Greek patriarch, under whose protection the Georgians had placed themselves. The church is very handsome, clean, and adorned with paintings. The chapel of St. James, where he is said to have been beheaded, is particularly rich. Opposite is a nunnery of the Armenians.

The Copts have their convent behind the church of the Holy Sepulchre. The Abyssinians have theirs in the same place. It contains a large collection of Ethiopic MSS., some historical, but most of them translations from the Bible and the Fathers.

The convent and church of the Syrians, called that of St. Marini or of St. Mary, is on the spot where St. Mary, the mother of St. Marini dwelt.

The Jews have only three synagogues, all in bad condition ; but I observed that they often have private meetings in the houses of rich individuals. It would be a great mistake to judge from these synagogues of the condition of the Jews in Jerusalem. As their numbers are never accurately reported,

they are also cunning enough to appear to the Turks, out-
wardly, as poor as possible.

Jerusalem has been distinguished by the bounty of the ca-
liphs, sultans, and other sovereigns, to whom it is indebted
for many mosques.   Private persons have likewise been liberal
in this manner.   But most of those mosques were formerly
Christian churches.   They are so numerous, that a very large
proportion is not used.

There are six baths in the city ; the water of one of them is
salt, and has a medicinal virtue.   The water which is drawn
during the day flows again in great abundance during the night.
All these baths are of ancient date.

On the Arabic Language ;. the difference between the written and vulgar Language, &c.

In Egypt as well as in Syria, Arabic is almost exclusively
spoken and understood.   Only in Maloula and Sidnaia, near
Damascus, the dialect is so different that it is considered to
be Syriac.   Turkish is spoken only by some civil officers and
soldiers, and the inhabitants of Scanderoon and Beilan.   The
Greek and Armenian monks speak their national languages, the
Latins the Italian.

As the difference between the Arabic written language of
the golden age of Arabic literature, from that now in use, is
greatly exaggerated, so is also the difference of that spoken in
various provinces, or in the several parts of the same province.   It is true we may perceive a considerable difference
in the grammar and syntax, and several words are adopted,
which are used but seldom in writing, or in a different sense.
But still the difference is not so great as is pretended.   A well-
informed Greek will never understand the works of his ancestors, without preparatory study ; but the Arab does, as I frequently convinced myself among the Bedouins in Egypt and
Syria, and the inhabitants of the towns and villages in both
provinces.   I was as much astonished at the ease with which
they read and commented upon Antar, Macrizi, Abulfeda,
&c. as they were at my acquaintance with the contents of those
works. It cannot excite surprise that some places have adopted
certain peculiarities, especially in the pronunciation.   This is
the same with all languages, and all the inhabitants testified
that it was so in a high degree in the different villages in
Egypt.   But according to my observations the difference is
not so great.   The Bedouins in the Delta and Middle Egypt
speak better than the villagers.   The peculiarities in the language of the several provinces are more important.

The Arab in Yemen is known to be the best that is spoken. Many words that are used by the best educated Arabs in Cairo are not employed there. They know only the more elegant forms of the written language.

In Jerusalem there are many words in daily use, different from those employed at Cairo, to designate the same objects.

There are likewise some diversities in the language of the coast towns of the villages, and especially of the Bedouins in Syria. However inconsiderable they may be, it would be important to know them, because in the peculiaries of dialect in the coast towns, we might perhaps find some remains of the Phœnician.

In Beirout they speak bad Arabic. On Lebanon they swallow many syllables. In Palestine no peculiar dialects can be distinguished : only the pronunciation of syllables and words is different. Thus in many parts *kaf* is pronounced like *ain*. In the villages about Samaria they generally speak slow, and their mode of speaking, as well as their whole exterior, has an appearance of sincerity ; but at the bottom they are rogues, inclined to revolt, and notorious robbers. The inhabitants of some villages about Gaza, drawl out most of their words in a singing tone, and the old people carry this to such an excess that one can hardly help laughing. At Jericho they speak quick, but have a very bad way of pronouncing the vowels, which are often hardly heard. The Bedouins on the Jordan and Dead Sea speak the Arabic better than the inhabitants of Jerusalem. Natural defects in speaking, as well as very ill habits, are unknown to them; but in general the Arabic spoken in Palestine is not considered as the best. The women generally drawl their words, especially in short phrases, and sing just like the Jewish women with us.

It has often been remarked that a knowledge of the comparisons and proverbs used in the language of the people, would be advantageous in the study of ancient writers. I did not meet with any thing particular in their comparisons and proverbs, they were such as are very common in the Oriental writers, especially poets ; and I am inclined to doubt whether any new and unknown ones would be discovered among them. This is another proof of the little difference between the written and the vulgar language.

In Syria and Egypt, the love of literature is confined to some Arabs in the capital cities, Cairo, Aleppo, Damascus, and Acre. In the other cities all my inquiries after MSS. were fruitless. I was assured that the MSS. of the historical kind were chiefly procured from Cairo, where every thing was to be had.

At Jerusalem I saw the history of Antar, in twenty-three octavo volumes, and also several copies of the Chronicle of Raschid. The largest library in Syria is at Acre. Ghezzar Pacha composed it of the library of the convent of St. Salvator, near Saida, of that of the Sheik Kairi, and that of the Mufti of Rama. It contains eight hundred and four numbers, but not so many different works. Thus there are several copies of the work on the Sects, and among the many collections of letters, several appear to be identical. Unfortunately the names of the authors are never specified in the catalogue which I have seen. There may be many unknown and interesting works in it; but it is very difficult to obtain permission to see them.

Not only the towns, but most of the villages, have schools; from which, however, the women are wholly excluded. In those of the Christians, as well as those of the Mahometans, only reading and writing are taught, and sometimes, in those of the Latin Christians, the Italian language. The latter likewise give religious instruction in the church on Sundays, by catechising; but the other Christian sects are as unacquainted with this mode as the Turks themselves. The children sit dispersed in the room on their hams; the master questions them in succession; the rest all read their lessons aloud, so that there is always a great noise in these schools. They write either with the *Kalaam* on polished paper, or with a stone on metal plates, or with a coloured pencil on a kind of tablet. The Mahometans write and read nothing but the Koran, and prayers that are filled with phrases taken from it. They are not communicative of either to the Christians. But the Imans write out copies of this book for the Musselmen, generally in four parts, and gain their livelihood partly by this occupation. The Christians read in their schools the Psalter, from copies printed on Mount Lebanon, or from MSS.

The following may serve as a proof of the ignorance of the clergy at Jerusalem. The contest of the several parties for the possession of the church of the Holy Sepulchre, or its chapel, is still carried on with much animosity. As the Greeks have the advantage of all the others, by expending large sums, and by intrigues, they also found means to get the better of them, by proving the justice of their claims from ancient documents. Among these there is one written in Neski character, which they ascribe to Omar, and by which he grants the church of the Holy Sepulchre to them and their posterity, as their property for ever. Even if they had not the fact against them, that in the seventh century there was no dispute about the church, the circumstance that the Neski character was wholly

unknown at that time, would suffice to prove this document to
be a forgery. Nevertheless they boast of it not only in Jerusalem and Damascus, but even in the Divan of Constantinople. The Armenian dragoman in the Divan, by a witty remark, caused the decision to be put off, when the Greeks
thought themselves already sure of the victory. When the
Greek dragoman affirmed that their rights to the church of the
Holy Sepulchre were founded upon firmans, according to
which their ancestors possessed it in the remotest times, he replied, that if those rights were to be enforced, the church of
St. Sophia must also be given up to them. This answer pleased
the Divan so well that the affair was adjourned.

All the Orientals have a propensity to superstition. As the
Christians have for certain misfortunes certain saints, whose
intercession they invoke, so have the Mahometans and Jews
certain formulæ which act as talismen, and these are written
in certain characters which only the initiated understand, who
by this means give them great importance. The Jews employ,
among others, what is called Kataba Lihona. Some Rabbis
are of opinion that it was invented by Kutai, on Mount Lebanon, and hence derives its name. Their superstition includes
the belief in ghosts, apparitions, &c. Thus for instance it is
said, that on the mountain, a quarter of a league north of Beil-
deras, a hen with her chickens sometimes appears, which
guards a treasure buried there.

The administration of justice is very simple in the East. The
judge does not even qualify himself for his office by many
years previous study. He studies his Koran and some Com-
mentaries, and at the most, the writings of some lawyers, and
interprets or perverts the Koran according to his own judgment. At Constantinople, where they are the best educated,
they are said not to enjoy any esteem, and to be more exposed
than others to contempt and ill usage; but as soon as they are
sent into the provinces they play the tyrant. Their decrees
are infallible. The judge hears both parties, puts questions,
makes objections, and decides verbally on the spot. In every
considerable place there is a judge, commonly for life, and
many of them, by natural sagacity and witty decisions, have
gained the attachment of those under their jurisdiction.; but
the majority have made themselves hated. Small transgressions are punished by them with imprisonment, and in
preference with a fine; greater ones with death, the loss
of an eye, or other member. They go about the town
to examine, according to their fancy, and if they any where
find a deficiency of weight or measure, they inflict pu-
nishment on the spot. They are under the Mufti at Constan-

tinople, who in appearance is independent of the Divan, though in fact all his actions are under its controul. It might be thought that by this independence of the Pacha, the despotism of the latter would be checked, but in general they do not pay attention to him.

The dervises are here quite naked, live at the expence of others, and enjoy uncontrolled liberty. They attack girls, and sometimes women, in the streets, and are even covered in the act by the pious Mahometans. At Jaffa one of them proceeded to such extremities with the Christian women, that the English consul Damian, yoked him to the wheel of a mill, like an ox, and made him draw till he promised never more to molest Christian women. At the festival of Easter, the dervise from Chalil, now living at Jerusalem, did violence to a Catholic woman of the Latin church. He had pulled off her head-dress in her room; she followed him to recover it, till he threw her down. On our journey to the Jordan we requested the governor strictly to inquire at whose instigation he had done it, for it was generally said that the Greeks had prompted him to this act of violence. The governor promised to inquire into the affair. They do with impunity what they please. If they are called to account, they answer, " *Schar Allah.* God put it into my head." The Mahometans highly esteem a child of such a dervise; they have free access to the harem, and are not responsible for any thing they do. They often beat the Christians, who are obliged to bear it patiently. Very strict Motsellams punish them by imprisonment.

Diseases in Palestine.

The small-pox still rages among children in the East, and no care is taken to inoculate them. At Jerusalem it is said not to be frequent. When I was at Nazareth there were many children infected with it. The Tertian ague is common in Judæa in the summer time. The coarse food, unripe fruit, the use of pepper in large quantities, bleeding, want of exercise, and the sulphureous exhalations from the Dead Sea, may be the chief causes of it. The Turks frequently complain of giddiness and momentary stupor, and yet will not refrain from the use of opium. Epilepsy is very rare, and the symptoms nearly the same as with us. Leprosy is more frequent. Many poor persons afflicted with that disorder live in huts on Mount Sion, secluded from the rest of the world. Some are likewise met with in the streets, asking alms.

The Christians generally indemnify themselves for their ri-

gorous fasting, by the use of brandy, which unhappily subjects
them at an early period of life to apoplexy. At Nazareth I
saw many old people afflicted with disorders in the eyes,
which may perhaps be caused by the heavy damp air that
comes from Lebanon. Fits of melancholy are seldom attended
with the same symptoms in Syria as among us.

The character of the inhabitants of the East, particularly
of the Mahometan, is serious ; he seldom laughs, and always
speaks with a certain gravity. A great misfortune can de-
press him extremely, and his discourse, as well as his writings,
may have the impression of a suddenly excited imagination,
but a permanent state of this kind is foreign to his character.
There is no want of persons who fancy themselves sick.
Many of the villagers especially, asked my advice, and, upon
an accurate examination, it appeared that nothing ailed
them. In general the native of the East is less susceptible
of disease than the native of the West. He is more inured to
hardship from his youth, always in the open air, accustomed
to simple food, and an enemy to all refinement. Yet they
seldom reach any great age, and those who grow old generally
die at about eighty. At Nazareth they spoke of a man one
hundred and four years old, as a most extraordinary phenomenon. It is said that strangers, especially Jews, who settle
here, are not long lived. It has been observed that the most
sickness is in October, November, and December; the most
births in July, August, and September ; and that most of the
women die who lie in at Jerusalem in July. In general
they have no midwives; and this alone is very unfortunate.
Immediately after the birth, they lace the body so tight, that
the patient can scarcely breathe. The violent heat of July
may increase the bad consequences of this practice. As most
of the diseases proceed from the stomach, which is weakened
by the immoderate use of coffee and tobacco, and the early
indulgence of the sexual propensity, emetics and laxatives
are generally prescribed. If the first dose of medicine does not
afford relief, they generally think it useless to continue it.

The number of births generally exceeds that of deaths ; the
plague alone reverses this proportion. The pilgrims generally
bring it from Cairo and Damascus, and is said to be proved by
repeated experience, that that coming from Damascus is far
less dangerous than that from Cairo.

It generally comes to Galilee in March or April, to Jerusa_
lem in May or June, but it seldom rages here. Since the
French invasion, when many persons were carried off, it has
appeared but twice in Galilee; but on one of these two occa-

sions, the fathers were confined to their convent for eleven months.

The hospital in the Latin convent, the only one in Jerusa-was quite empty in 1821. The laboratory connected with it, is amply stored with every thing necessary, and renowned for the balsam which is made there. It is here alone that the genuine balsam can be had, which is compounded of fifty-five different ingredients, some of which are very expensive. The confidence of the Turks in the fathers and their medicine, is evinced by their taking the medicine without requiring them to taste it first. They are more employed as physicians than any others, either natives or foreigners. Vitus Filukka, a German father who came there about three years ago, is a particular favourite. These fathers make use of this opportunity to bap-tize any one who is near dying, without the knowledge of himself or his relations, and they are very proud of their suc-cess in this way. I know one who affirms he has baptized eighty in this manner, and was often in the greatest embarrass-ment when the patient seemed likely to recover.

Amusements of the Orientals.

Passion week was very lively in Jerusalem, because a fes-tival of the Mahometans occurred at the same time. It coin-cided with the time at which they annually make a pilgrimage to Vadi Musa, where Moses is said to be buried. What they call Moses' stone is found there, which burns like a coal, with-out consuming, and smells like asphaltum. This pilgrimage is made with a great deal of noise. The people flock out of the gate Setti Mariam. The women form lines on each side. Some men stand together in groups, and amuse themselves with firing muskets; but the most ride in different troops to this valley. Each of these troops keeps up an incessant firing, those who are well mounted, shew their skill in horsemanship ; they sing, and most have instrumental music, the only object of which is to make as much noise as possible. I have never seen the Mahometans so merry. Out of the other gates there were likewise numbers in their holiday clothes, but most were before this gate, because the road leads from it to Vadi Musa.

A very common amusement of the boys is the simple music of a tambourine with bells, to which monkies dressed in rags are made to dance. Grown up people frequently look on, and often too amuse themselves with playing at some game in the coffee-houses ; but most commonly they smoke tobacco either there or in their divan, drink coffee, and speak a few words to each other. Customs derived from antiquity, either in this or other respects, are in vain sought among them.

The women in the East have no amusement but when the weather is fine in the afternoon to visit the church-yards, where they sometims pray over the graves of their friends, sometimes converse together, sometimes abuse those who pass by, or look on, while the children are clambering up the trees. It is probable that acquaintances may make appointments, and take the opportunity of conversing on their domestic affairs. It is thought highly indecorous for a man to approach them, even at a distance. When the well of Jeremiah overflowed, the people flocked out of Jerusalem to it; but nobody dared to go near because some women had stationed themselves close by it.

Throughout the East decorum and modesty are most strictly maintained, but the manner in which it is done is very different in different places. In Chalil no woman dares unveil before a man, even were he her own brother, without hazarding the lives of both. A man dare not shew himself in a bye street, without exposing himself to the most dangerous suspicion. The bazar alone is publicly open to every body. In other cities, as Gaza, Jaffa, Jerusalem and Nahlous, they are not so strict; but the women always have their faces covered, none dare speak face to face with any but their relations; their dress is frightful, inconvenient and dirty. In the country, and even in several towns, they are less rigorous in this respect, and the women cover their faces, either half only, or not at all, when a man comes towards them; but they always live separate. At Jaffa I lodged in a house where there were many women in the lower story. Whenever I entered the house they ran from their work into the room, though I avoided even looking at them. The consequence of this separation is, that instances of unchastity are rare. The penalty of death, which is the inevitable consequence, has still more effect.

In the country their dress consists of a pair of wide trowsers, which are often very handsomely ornamented below, of a long blue shirt, fastened round the breast with a girdle, and often of a large handkerchief, which hangs down so as almost to cover the whole person. At Richa they have a long blue dress tied round the body and open before. The Christian women differ from the Mahometans in wearing a white handkerchief before the face, whereas the others commonly wear a black one. A number of gold or silver coins strung together are often bound round the head by way of ornament. They are very fond of black eyes and dye them. They express joy by a monotonous song, the whole text of which is lu, lu, &c.

The men wear in Galilee breeches, a wide shirt, and over it a short coat without sleeves; and in bad weather a large cloak, which looks more like a blanket. On their heads they wear a long red cap.

The wedding is one of the greatest festivals among the Oriental Christians. The whole village, and in towns, the greater part of the congregation, and many persons who do not belong to them, assemble and dance, i. e. leap before each other, clapping their hands, and then eat rice and meat. The hospitality of the Orientals is not much commended at present, however sacred to them the duty appears, of kindly providing strangers gratis with all necessaries. They are so little able to hide their poverty and distress, that you willingly indemnify them for their expense and trouble. The schismatic Greeks are remarkable for their cunning in this respect. The khans, of which so many are seen in a dilapidated condition, recal the memory of better times. Even the last remnant of them, the custom of keeping, in all the high roads, reservoirs filled with water, to which the nearest village is bound; is still retained only in a few places. I often expressed my dissatisfaction at this to the Arabs, who always answered, " where are those happy times now ? where shall we now find hospitality ?"

Their domestic mode of life forms a contrast with ours. They shave the head and let the beard grow; we shave the beard, and let the hair of the head grow. With them it would be unpolite to uncover the head in the presence of an acquaintance; with us it is unpolite not to do it. We sit on chairs, eat at tables, and sleep in beds; they sit, eat and sleep on the ground. We eat with knives, forks, and spoons, from plates and dishes; they with their fingers from one common dish. Our dishes and liquors are compounded; theirs plain. We have numerous wants; the Orientals very few. We travel in carriages; they ride. We love and seek exercise; the Orientals never take any without a certain object. We love change; they uniformity. A dress which was common only thirty years back is ridiculous among us; with them the same dresses, manners and customs prevail that were in use thousands of years ago. Our domestic animals are as effeminate as ourselves; those of the Orientals are able to endure the greatest hardships. They observe their fasts very strictly; we less so, and in quite a different manner.

In general the Orientals are more honest, they never steal; the Occidentals are more given to cheat: the former proceed more quickly to act, the latter are more considerate. They transact every thing publicly; with us there is no end of mystery. With us the fair sex reign in the family and in society, and are allowed to show their charms; there they see no company, and are obliged to go veiled from head to foot.

With us the bride receives a dowry from her father, there he is paid a considerable sum for her.

On the whole, the physical and moral character of the East, reposes on principles which are in the main, the same as they were some thousand years ago, and which make a permanent contrast to those of the West. In the East, religion is the observance of certain prescribed rules. Our administration of justice is regulated by wise, natural, and positive laws; theirs governed by the will of a despot, to whom every thing belongs, who can dispose at pleasure of the lives of his subjects, as his own property. For some thousands of years one tyrant has made room for another, and every one revels by the right of the strongest, on the possessions of his subjects.

In vain do we seek in the list of their sovereigns for benefactors like Sextus V. Henry IV. Frederick II. and Maria Theresa, whom every Italian, Frenchman, Prussian and Austrian names with profound respect and ardent love, and in whose reigns he might find the ideal of a golden age. The Oriental is proud of individual liberty, and maintains it by the revenge of blood; but then he renounces civil freedom. We willingly allow our individual liberty to be controuled by wise laws, but live happy in the enjoyment of civil freedom. Our life is more active; that of the Orientals more passive. Our mode of living is refined and changeable; theirs simple and permanent. Among us prevails an impulse towards great civilization; among them a tendency to barbarism.

For centuries a curse has rested on these countries, which formerly contained rich and powerful cities, the environs of which were covered with innumerable villages, cultivated fields, and crowded roads. The riches of every climate flowed to them; in their walls opulence and luxury reigned, and their streets were animated by the incessant bustle of commerce and art, and the sounds of festivity and joy. These numerous blocks of marble that lie scattered around, once decked the sumptuous palace, these mighty columns of marble and granite, once enhanced the splendour of the imperial hall, or the awful majesty of the temple. These dreary places covered with unseemly rubbish, which savage beasts have now chosen for their abode, were once the resort of a busy multitude who flocked hither from every part of south western Asia.

THE END.

LONDON:

SHACKELL AND ARROWSMITH, JOHNSON'S-COURT, FLEET-STREET.

A

VOYAGE

IN THE

SOUTH SEAS,

IN

THE YEARS 1812, 1813, AND 1814.

WITH

PARTICULAR DETAILS

OF THE

GALLIPAGOS AND WASHINGTON ISLANDS.

By CAPTAIN DAVID PORTER,

Of the American Frigate, The Essex.

WITH THREE ENGRAVINGS.

LONDON:

PUBLISHED BY SIR RICHARD PHILLIPS & Co.

BRIDE-COURT, BRIDGE-STREET.

1823.

[*Price 3s. 6d. sewed, or 4s. in boards.*]